POSITIVELY
YOU!

POSITIVELY YOU!

Jinger Heath

Change Your Thinking, Change Your Life

Golden Books
New York

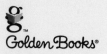

888 Seventh Avenue

New York, NY 10106

Copyright © 1998 by Jinger Heath

All rights reserved, including the right of reproduction in whole or in part in any form.

Golden Books® and colophon are trademarks of Golden Books Publishing Co., Inc.

Designed by James Reyman Studio

Manufactured in the United States of America

10 9 8 7 6 5 4 3 2

Library of Congress Cataloging-in-Publication Data

Heath, Jinger.

    Positively you! : change your thinking, change your life / Jinger Heath.

      p. cm.

    ISBN 0-307-44049-4

      1. Women—United States—Psychology.   2. Women—United States—Attitudes.   3. Self-esteem in women—United States.   4. Self-confidence—United States.   I. Title.

HQ1206.H425   1998

646.7'0082—dc21   97-33553

                                        CIP

Acknowledgments

MY DEEPEST THANKS AND APPRECIATION TO MY MENTOR, BEST friend, and soul mate, Richard Heath. I thank you for your love, morality, and integrity, and your commitment to honoring any new direction I have chosen to travel. Richard, thank you for being by my side and making me your bride. God has so richly blessed me with you.

To my precious mother, Wyanell, who taught me to enjoy and love people and to risk traveling down difficult roads. Mom, you never had an easy road to travel, yet you have shown me by example how to overcome and grow.

To all four of my incredible children, Robert, Richard, Michael, and Brittany Elizabeth, who are unique, special individuals. Each of you has taught me as much about life as I have taught you.

To all the Dallas BeautiControl team and the fifty thousand Consultants who travel a new road every day and inspire me to grow and learn.

Especially to the 550 BeautiControl Directors, who stand out as the best of the best and whose life stories epitomize what Positively You! is all about.

A standing ovation to my friend and literary agent, Jan Miller, who is an absolute genius!

To my editor, Bob Asahina, whose talent in the world of publishing is unsurpassed. Thank you for believing in me and wanting this book for women.

Acknowledgments

To all the terrific people at Golden Books, who are setting the new standards for publishing with their creative, caring, quality approach to each project.

A special thanks to Walter and Maxwell for contributing to this book and my journey.

To my friends who have tolerated my very busy life, who have believed in me and influenced me in so many positive ways. Thank you for being there for me even though I can't be with you as much as I'd like. I love you, Sandy Alford, Mary Lynn Garth, Sydney Huffines, Bay Innamorati, Denise Lites, Nancy Marcus, Judy Messina, Aileen Pratt, Annette Simmons, and Jill Smith.

To my personal assistant, Beverly Duckworth, without whom I would not be sane. Bev, thank you for typing this book countless times and never complaining. Thank you for helping me do what I do best, by handling my busy business and personal life. Your warm, patient, and friendly voice on the phone blesses everyone who calls.

To my mother, Wyanell Clark, my husband, Richard White Heath,
and our four children, Robert, Richard, Michael, and
Brittany Elizabeth

Contents

Contents

Introduction
The Power of Your Dreams

Stop Postponing Your Life and Start Living It

As women, we have all felt that terrifying sense of inadequacy.
We have wondered if we can find real-life solutions to improve
ourselves. We have lived such conforming lives for so long that
many of us think it is too late for us to change.

We are wrong!

JUST FOR A MOMENT, TAKE A BREATH, CLEAR YOUR MIND, AND
try to answer this question: **What would it feel like to totally
believe in yourself again . . . ?** To know that you had the inner
strength to change whatever it is you wanted to change in
your life? What would it feel like to once again embrace
your dreams and to actively work at living them out instead
of daydreaming about them? What would it feel like to re-

discover the potential that for years may have been lying dormant, buried somewhere in your unconscious?

Does it feel uncomfortable for you to think about answering these questions? Does it feel foreign to imagine a life in which you no longer have to worry about the past or the future but you can instead live in the moment?

Again, try to clear your mind of any doubt or skepticism. Take another deep breath. And now answer this question: **What would it feel like if you could totally believe in yourself again—if you could experience that glorious, bone-deep feeling of hope that you may not have had in a long, long time?**

I'm not asking you to pretend to believe! I'm not resorting here to some self-help rhetoric to get you to make more "positive" statements about yourself. I'm talking about really believing in yourself, plain and simple. I'm talking about living with such passion that time seems to race by joyously rather than drag along. I'm talking about a life of wonderful creativity, in which you develop greater confidence in yourself, discover boundless energy, and find deeper serenity than you ever thought was possible. True self-love gives you the permission to accept all the unique and special qualities about you and only you!

How a Dream Begins

LET ME TELL YOU A STORY ABOUT AN AMAZING EVENT that happens every summer on a huge stage in Nashville, Tennessee. The event is called "Celebration," and it's the annual gathering of women who are associated with a cosmetics company known as BeautiControl. In 1981, my husband, Dick, and I took the risk of our lives, taking out a $600,000 loan, putting ourselves up to our eyeballs in debt, and then telling our closest friends and family that we were going to create a company that would change the lives of thousands of women throughout America.

"Oh, come on," people would tell us. "Another cosmetics company? How can a cosmetics company change anyone's life?"

Some of our friends literally laughed at our plan. "Jinger," they said, "you have children to raise. You and Dick have no money, no partners, and no employees. What are you doing?"

"There is no company like the one we're starting," I would reply. "We're going to give women a chance to reach inside themselves and do things with their lives that they never thought were possible."

My friends would look at me and wonder what could be going through my mind. But I never stopped talking—or believing. "I know there are thousands upon thousands of women out there who have lost their self-confidence," I would say. "All we're going to do is help them touch that long-neglected strength that lies inside them. That's our dream. **Dick and I know this company can become the vehicle for women who want to believe in themselves again but don't know how.**"

It sounded good, didn't it? You may be thinking, a little too good. Perhaps the dream was a little too rosy? Here we were, a little-known couple in Dallas, Texas, announcing that we were going to create a dynamic cosmetics company and, in the process, give women who joined us a chance to unleash the powerful, untapped energy inside them. Come on. Surely we had to be kidding ourselves!

In fact, when we started our little cosmetics business, there were over one hundred other companies in America manufacturing and selling cosmetics. The $600,000 loan we had to take out, just to get the company on its already faltering feet, was about the same amount of money many other cosmetics companies spent every couple of weeks on advertising alone.

Dick and I, however, absolutely believed that if we provided a lucrative opportunity for women, we could build a great company. All we had to do was show those who joined us how to break through their own fears and insecurities. **All we had to do was get them to believe in themselves!**

A prominent businessman once asked my husband, "Dick, why don't you set up your company so that your products are sold in stores and you pay some employees by commission to sell them?"

"You mean, like almost every other cosmetics company?" Dick asked.

"That's right," said the businessman.

"Because we don't want to invest our dollars in buildings and advertising," Dick said. "We're going to put our dollars into our salespeople. Each of these women will be her own 'store,' so to speak. They'll choose how much they work and how much they make. Their income will be limited only by their vision."

The businessman was stunned. "That's crazy. You're going to bank your entire company on a group of women who have had no training, no business experience? How are you going to control them?"

"We're not going to control anyone," Dick said patiently. "We're going to show our salespeople how to believe in themselves."

The power of believing in yourself! The concept seemed so obvious, so clichéd, so pat. Could it really be the foundation of a company?

We knew it could. We set up our business as a company in

which our saleswomen (known as Consultants and Directors) would operate as independent salespeople. They would work out of their own homes, they would decide how often they worked and how much money they made. And we made sure there was no cap whatsoever on how much money they could earn. The more their sales rose, and the more the women shared their career opportunity with others, the richer they'd become.

Of course, we were under no illusion that this would be easy. We knew we were setting out to do a lot more than just train women to sell cosmetics. From my own experience, I knew that some of the women we would try to help would have little self-esteem. Many would not feel confident expressing themselves or displaying their talents. We knew we would have to give many women the courage to change—women who desperately wanted out of their unhappy nine-to-five jobs, women who were sick of trying to climb the male-dominated corporate ladder, women who wanted to spend more time with their families at home but felt they couldn't get out of their dead-end jobs for fear of losing money.

And, so, we literally rolled up our sleeves and went to work. My fantasy of becoming a so-called glamorous cosmetics queen quickly dissolved. I came to the office and stuffed envelopes, swept the floors, cleaned the bathrooms, painted the old company machinery, put creams in jars, and tried to find the time to create new cosmetics and other products that I knew American women wanted and needed. On top of that, I began traveling the country, speaking to our Consultants or those thinking about becoming Consultants, talking about the possibilities that lay before them, the exhilaration of achieving not just financial success, but also the "inner" success that rarely comes to women, who often are pulled in so many directions.

Dick and I did what we could to keep the creditors away, to keep the banks from calling our loans, and to find new investors to keep us afloat. And, slowly, we started to grow—and grow. Women began to hear about us. They heard that we had created a company in which a woman's success was dependent on her own motivation, not based on whether her male boss liked her. They heard they could make as much money as they wanted and no longer had to be stuck in a corporate world where women made only 76 cents for every dollar a man made. And they heard they could set their own hours, giving them the freedom and flexibility to pick up their children from school at the end of a day (as a mom myself, I knew that this was so important) or to stop working early enough to make a family dinner. Besides income and prestige, our company was giving women the long-needed balance in their lives that they had been sorely missing.

We might have been the new kids on the block, but it wasn't long before cosmetics giants began to copy our products and our sales techniques. We were both flattered and amazed at how we really were changing the face of an industry. We changed the way women were treated when they joined a selling organization. We didn't ask them to be cheerleaders. We gave women the tools they needed to sell and to believe in themselves.

By 1987, BeautiControl was listed as one of the one hundred fastest-growing small companies in America by *Business-Week* magazine, and *Glamour* magazine later honored me by naming me one of the Top Ten Outstanding Working Women for 1989. *Mirabella* listed me as one of America's one thousand most influential women. My cosmetics and fashion makeover seminars around the country were drawing more than one thousand women a session. Out of nowhere, we had become one of the largest companies in our field, with a sales force of more than fifty thousand Consultants and Directors. And as we approach the end of the 1990s, we will be surpassing more than $140 million in annual retail sales.

As a result, we now invite our sales force to Nashville or Dallas every summer for Celebration—our national convention. It is a frenzy of joy, of shouting and hugging and recognition. We give away thousands of dollars' worth of cars, trips, and diamonds to our top women. As spine-tingling music blares out of a booming sound system and spotlights sweep across the room, these women walk across the stage to be honored like movie stars at the Academy Awards.

But what we are celebrating is not just our saleswomen's financial achievements. We are celebrating what they have become as human beings. I must confess that I feel very proud at Celebration, for this is the time when my own dream comes true. My dream in life has been to share with other women some of the tools I have acquired in my own often-frustrating struggle to believe in myself.

Today, I realize that those experiences were like "gifts"— gifts that I can use to help others achieve a new outlook on their own lives. It always flabbergasts and amazes me each year when I am introduced at our Celebration opening assembly to the three thousand–plus women who are there. As I walk out on stage, some even stand on their chairs and let out high-pitched screams so stunning that you think you might be in the middle of a revolution. The first five minutes I'm on stage, it is hard for me to see because so many people have rushed to the front to take photographs with flashing cameras.

Inevitably, I am so overwhelmed by the reaction that I can

hardly speak. Deep emotions well up inside me. It's almost as if I'm having an out-of-body experience, in which I step back from the whole scene and think, **"Why am I here? Am I really on stage in front of women who want to hear from me? Is it me they are all cheering for? Am I in the wrong place?"**

As I stand there, I think back on my own life. I think about my childhood in West Texas, which was nothing like an Ozzie-and-Harriet life. As a child of a used car dealer and a hardworking mom, I had to become responsible for myself at an early age. I spent summers working in maize fields. Far from a "cosmetics queen," I was a bucktoothed, short, over-weight teenager who tried every diet imaginable to lose weight. As I got older, I became obsessed with creating the right exterior image, trying to look good on the outside as a shell to cover my insecurities and fears that made me ache on the inside. I lived with a chronic sense of disappointment in myself, longing to change but not knowing exactly what to do. All I knew to do in order to feel better about myself was to achieve and "do" more. As long as I did more, then I believed I was proving my worth and value.

And as I stand in front of that crowd of women at Celebration, I think back on a time in my life, before we started our company, when I was so full of self-doubt, when I felt like a failure as a wife and as a woman—so overwhelmed by a sense of depression that I checked myself into a hospital. I lay in a hospital bed for days, barely able to talk to my family or my closest friends. I had hit bottom. I realized I had to change something—or some behavior. I had to learn to think differently, or I knew I wouldn't be able to function or even stay sane. **I had to change.**

It was at that point I made a conscious decision to alter my life forever, to get rid of the emptiness and despair and to make every moment of my life count, to embrace the things that matter most, and to try to touch others so that they, too, could choose to change.

For years, I searched for answers. I realized I was going to have to face the negative side of myself and learn to dispose of it. I was going to have to say good-bye to fears and anxieties that had been afflicting me since early childhood. I needed to learn why I could not believe in myself—why my inner engine kept misfiring and why I could not steer myself onto the right road in my journey through life.

And only then did I begin to touch that glorious part inside me that was so full of life and creativity. That's right, I learned again to believe in myself. I began to live out my dreams. And that is why, at every Celebration, I make sure to say somewhere in my speech to our women, "This is the day your dreams can come true. What the mind can conceive and believe, it can achieve!"

Discovering a Life of Meaning

TODAY, OUR COMPANY IS ONE OF THE GREAT SUCCESS STORIES in American business. Besides an array of new moisturizers, skin care products, and color cosmetics, to the best of my knowledge, we hold one of just two patents in the world for alpha hydroxy products. We have created a body sculpting cream that has been lauded in a scientific journal for its ability to reduce fatty deposits and cellulite. We produce the finest line of vitamins, supplements, and weight-loss products available today. Indeed, we have gone to great lengths to improve the lives of women by showing them how to look and feel better about their physical appearance.

But that's not why I have written this book. Nor have I written this book to persuade you to go into cosmetic sales or to join our company in order to make your life better. That's hardly my intention at all.

Instead, the origin for this book came from the response I receive from people who travel to Nashville each summer to witness Celebration for themselves. Financial analysts, chief executive officers of other companies, psychologists, consultants, and even a few, sometimes cynical university professors come to study the women of our company and watch them walk across the stage to win awards and be recognized for the hundreds of thousands of dollars they have earned that year. These visitors sit there, mesmerized by the women's charm, confidence, and charisma. They watch the thousands of women in the audience laughing, crying, and cheering—clearly transported by an invisible power that runs through our company.

And, after Celebration, these visitors come up to Dick or me and ask, "Where did these women come from? How did you find women who are so driven, so motivated?"

I smile and tell them the stories of our company's women. Pointing out some of our top salespeople—women who have now earned millions but who were once almost too shy to speak when they first joined the company. I point out individuals whose lives today are filled with ambition and purpose but who not long ago may have felt isolated, alone, afraid, or trapped in an abusive situation.

The truth is that some of these women have come from environments no different from those of you who are reading this book. The majority of them had no experience in business, they possessed no public speaking skills, and some didn't know how to set a goal or how to begin to start their own business. You would be surprised at some of the stories

I could tell you about women who are very successful today. Before they decided to change the course of their lives, many felt trapped. Some felt as if they were drowning. Some were desperate to salvage some happiness out of their unfulfilled lives.

You and I know what that feels like, don't we? We all have felt that scary sense of inadequacy. We all have wondered if we could find any real-life solutions to improve ourselves. Many of us have lived such conforming lives for so long that we think it is too late for us to change.

We are wrong!

We, as women, can do something for ourselves. We can beat back those destructive attitudes that seem to undermine our greatest qualities. We can rediscover the best parts of our personalities and recapture our creative energy to change our lives for the better. We can join together as a sisterhood of women, traveling with each other on a journey to self-discovery. **We can share with one another how we have survived those very difficult twists in the road and how we have kept from driving off a cliff.**

I know some of you reading this book have spent years feeling that you have lost your way emotionally. You may think that life has become like a treadmill—the same old thing, day after day. The days may be filled with a nameless anxiety that you really can't explain. Or, you may realize that you are living, at best, with a sense of tolerance or complacency rather than with joy and the thrilling possibility of success. You may know that you were born with so much potential, yet you wonder where all that potential has gone. At the very time in American history when opportunities for women are increasing, many women wonder why they still feel trapped by their own anxieties.

But trust me on this. *If I can change, you can, too.* That's why I

have written this book—to share with you my stories, and the stories of other women I know, who learned how to turn their lives around.

Please, let's be clear about something. If your goal is to read a book that's only going to teach you how to be a better career woman, then you've got the wrong book. The women who joined our company didn't transform their lives by memorizing some sales and business techniques. What these women learned to do was to really believe in themselves. How? They learned that they didn't have to be subjugated to the negative attitudes or expectations of others. They learned to let go of the burden of their pasts. They learned that a meaningful life comes from what they give, not just what they receive.

Those tools are what I most want to share with you—so you will realize that you can accomplish anything you want, whether it is to advance yourself in a career, gain self-esteem, develop deeper and more solid relationships, or just meet the everyday challenges of adult life. I want to encourage you to stop postponing your life and start living it. And I mean living the good life. By that, I don't mean mansions and world travel—although if that's what you really want, you can have it. Ultimately, I'm talking about achieving a life you love, where you jump out of bed excited about the day ahead, where you know your life is in balance and you are making a mark on the world around you.

Getting Your Wheels in Motion

As you read this book, you are going to discover that I have a tendency to make lots of car references. Remember, my father was a used car dealer, and when I was a little girl, I spent a lot of time in used cars. So I learned early what a car "out of alignment" felt like, how the wheels vibrated and how the steering wheel would wobble if the car needed balance. Daddy taught me that if a car was only slightly out of alignment, it would pull you in a direction that you didn't want to go. If it pulled to the right, for example, then each and every other process of driving was affected. He taught me that if the parts of your car's engine were not in tune, then it was only a matter of time before you would be hit with costly repairs. When you've got an untuned engine and unbalanced wheels, you don't have much control over when and where you travel.

As silly as this sounds, I eventually began to equate my own life with a car that needed tuning and balancing. I saw myself as a car trying to get up to speed on life's highway, headed in the proper direction, aiming for the right destination. As an adult, it didn't take me long to realize that I wasn't driving a very good car—my life felt out of balance and alignment all too often. The most frustrating thing was when I would try to rebalance and realign myself, I'd end up hitting even more curbs and be in greater need of repair. I didn't know how to fix myself when I was broken. I struggled with being the joyful, fulfilled person I knew I was meant to be. As you'll read later in this book, what I tried was to look good on the outside, working overtime to be the most attractive and charming girl in the room, believing that if I looked "in control," then my life would be in control. What I was doing was basically the same thing my daddy would do to sell a used car. He'd give the car a shiny $99 paint job and do a quick steam-clean of the engine so that the car looked as if it were in great shape. But it was too costly to make the engine better. Although I was really good at creating an image of who I was on the outside, my internal engine kept getting clogged.

The fact is that it took me years to learn how to fix my

inner engine and keep it tuned so I could embark on any journey. It took even longer to finally learn how to balance my life so that I could prevent myself from constantly swerving and running off the road as my journey progressed.

This is my hope for you. I hope you can reach that point in your life where you know your engine (your inner self) is solid for the long haul, and you no longer have to worry about future twists and turns in the road. Obstacles that once blocked your progress will turn out to be small hurdles you will be able to get around easily. **And the biggest payoff of all? You will realize you are driving down the road you have chosen. You will be living your own dreams, not the dreams chosen for you by someone else.**

And it's all because you will have learned again to believe in yourself.

Don't Expect Pollyanna

BEFORE WE TURN THE PAGE, LET ME PROMISE YOU, I AM NO Pollyanna. There's no pretending that I am going to give you a magic potion or one of those instant fix-a-flat kits that don't really work in the long run. Nor am I going to give you one more self-help manual that is just going to tell you to say, "I can do it! I am a worthy person!" While I believe with every fiber of my being that each of us is a worthwhile person—and while I believe that affirmations do work, what we need most are permanent tools to keep our lives in balance and harmony. Or as my daddy would say, we need tools for our engines and good jacks to change our tires. And we need clear maps for our long journeys.

So get ready to start your engines! **Just by getting moving again, you are headed toward your dreams.** And, remember, no dream you cherish is too grand or too insignificant. No arena you strive to excel in is too large or too small. And do not be afraid of the changes that are destined to come into your life. The one constant in this universe is change. Just as we learn to expect curves in a road, we must learn to expect and embrace changes that lie ahead.

I have now spent most of my adult life helping other women make their dreams come true. I also have made my own dreams come true. And what I have found, in my own story and in the stories of other women, is that the process of change requires some hard work and a great amount of commitment, but it is not complicated or confusing, and it doesn't need to take a long time. Indeed, the distance between your reach and your grasp is not all that great. I see it over and over with the women who join our company—some of whom are ordinary women who learn new skills, draw upon their inner strength, and ultimately discover just how capable they are in all areas of their life. They learn the great secret that we all have to learn: that success on the outside starts with success on the inside. They have retuned those powerful engines that had been idling inside them, balanced their wheels, and in turn they have revolutionized their lives.

You're going to find yourself in these pages. We're first going to shine a spotlight on your inner engine so that we can find where it needs tuning. As you might have guessed, the clogs in our engines have been there for years and years, and we often have to go back in our pasts to clean them out. Then we're going to learn to unload some of the baggage that's been weighing down the trunks of our cars for far too long.

Next we'll come up with a way to rev up our engines again. We're going to look at each wheel on your car and make sure they are all rolling together, balanced and aligned so that every facet of your life is moving forward, smoothly and with ease! If one wheel of your life is to be good at your job, but the other wheels—such as your family or your relationship with yourself—are not moving well, then something may need to be rotated or even replaced. You will be able to begin changing your self (or your behavior) immediately by using the straightforward techniques found in this book—techniques that have been followed by other successful self-changers.

I am very, very excited about where we're going. The fact that you are holding this book in your hands shows you have the desire to do something for yourself—that you have the desire to find the tools to build a better framework for your life. **The journey we're about to take is a glorious one, leading to horizons you never knew existed.** You have nothing to lose but some unneeded shaking and wobbling.

So join me in a journey that is exciting, fulfilling, nurturing, and, most of all, comforting.

I

Who Are You and Where Are You Going?

Learning to Believe in Yourself Again

Do you know what you really want your life to be like a year from now? What about five years from now? Now ask yourself the tough question: Are you sure you are on the right road to get you there?

The Road to Nowhere

How Did You Get So Lost in Life?

Before we figure out how to get on the right road in life, we've
got to figure out how to get off the wrong one. And we have to
figure out why we got on the wrong road in the first place.
Otherwise, even if someone gives us good directions to find the
right road, we'll end up on another wrong road anyway.

IF YOU'VE READ A LOT OF SELF-HELP BOOKS—AND HEAVEN
knows, I've read them all—then you've probably never seen a
chapter like the one you're about to read. This is the chapter
that explains how crazy our lives as women can become.

Many writers and speakers will try to make you think that
all you have to do to get your life on track is ignore the
source of your emotional problems and just start feeling

positive about yourself. They'll do a big cheerleading act and tell you, "You can change," but they won't try to get you to think about why you respond so negatively to many situations in life.

Well, it's time for us to shoot straight with one another. And it's also time for us as women to support one another. I have memorized and repeated more "positive thinking" slogans and aphorisms than you can imagine. I keep a book of affirmations on the back of my potty. And, believe me, they are great. But they are great *now*. All the affirmations in the world weren't helping me some years ago when I didn't understand why I was acting the way I was and when I didn't have the tools to change my behavior and improve my life.

Over the years, I have met so many women who I know could be so accomplished and so happy, yet who clearly are frustrated by their place in the world. You would not believe the number of women I've met in business who felt hopeless and overwhelmed. In many ways, these women are typical of women all over America. They wonder what happened to their own hopes and dreams and why they got put on the back burner. Many have lost their feelings of self-confidence. Some have lost touch with their wonderful feminine spirit. It's as if they live on a kind of "automatic pilot"—going through the motions of work or homemaking every day and never really taking pleasure in what is going on around them. It's like they aren't present in the here and now.

Almost daily, I meet women who have no idea where they are going, what road they're headed down, and how long their engine (their mental sanity) can last. Some are housewives who feel their special skills are becoming rusty while they raise their children. Others are career women in various fields who feel their careers are devouring their lives instead of feeding them. There are some single women who don't know how to love themselves because they feel incomplete at not having found the right man. There are married women who find themselves beaten down emotionally, sometimes physically, by mates who have little self-esteem of their own. And there are so many of us women who have been programmed from birth to feel that we aren't capable of a successful life.

Do You Feel Destined for Unhappiness?

W HAT'S JUST AS BAFFLING IS THAT THE ANSWERS ARE not becoming any clearer despite the fact that so many of us have spent years in the endless search for "something more" in life. We have tried every conceivable new path. We have followed the bliss, attempted to take the road less traveled, searched hard for our inner child. We've filled out all the magazine questionnaires promising to reveal what to do with our lives. We've read books advising us to work hard pleasing others and we've read books encouraging us to work hard pleasing only ourselves.

Yet we keep losing in the same ways, year after year. Why?

Why is it that we are living in the most successful society ever known—a society filled with remarkable accomplishments and constant new advances in technology and engineering—and yet so many of us feel plagued with the idea that we are destined for dullness?

Maybe we're confused about what success is. Why, in particular, are so many women still unsure about the way to handle their strong ambitions and their enormously powerful desire to be wonderful wives and mothers? And why do more and more of us seem to be losing our ability to look inside ourselves in order to find our inner core, our spiritual resonance, that special spark that can make our lives so important?

When I look around at our world, I wonder just how many women really know what it means to believe in themselves, to really love and cherish every fiber of their own being. So many women have made top priorities pleasing others, being attractive to others, or caring for others. They have learned to do just about everything except truly care for, nurture, believe in, and love themselves. They don't know what it means to experience a life that is well lived.

While reading one of my self-improvement books, I learned that in the 1950s, there were thirty-six distinct systems of psychotherapy used by psychologists and psychiatrists. Today, there are more than four hundred! The point is that no matter where you turn, you will find somebody with some new theory claiming he or she can really make the difference in your life. And if you've searched as I have, you can be tempted by any one of these people who promise to lead you out of the swamps of mediocrity and into the promised land of well-being. Indeed, you can spend the rest of your life "shopping" for psychological theories instead of attempting to seek an identity all your own.

Doctors say that between two and six times as many women as men are diagnosed as suffering from depression. Among women, anxiety is like the common cold, ready to strike at any moment. It's like the disease without a name. So many unexpressed feelings have built up inside us and made us feel crazy in all sorts of ways. Some of us find ourselves boiling underneath with resentment about the way our lives have turned out. Others of us apparently decide to spend the rest of our lives living with frustration rather than searching for any deeper sense of joy. Like dutiful daughters, some of us try to hide our feelings by leading what on the outside appear to be tidy, unchallenging lives. Others of us stay as busy as possible, refusing to stop moving—because if we do, we will have to face the fact that we don't really know who we are anymore. And then there are those of us who turn to an array of escapes to handle our misery. We indulge ourselves in various temporary mood changers, from a package of chocolate cookies, to alcohol, even to excessive exercise.

One woman I met who had just joined our company told me, "Jinger, I seem to sleep so much. I don't know why I should be tired. My house isn't that hard to clean. The children are at school all day. It's not the work of being a housewife that's got me down. I just don't feel alive."

Now let me stop for a second. I realize there is someone who is reading this page and saying, "Hold on. I'm not overly depressed. I don't have huge problems. Granted, I feel unsettled, and I know I'm not entirely fulfilled. But it's not like I'm really suffering."

There are so many of us women who have created what I call "comfort zones"—lifestyles that might not be really satisfying but are too comfortable for us to give up in order to seek true fulfillment. We believe we can go for a long, long time in this zone. Many of us think we can live a life of coping rather than one of growing.

Frankly speaking, a lot of us can spend the rest of our lives in our comfort zones and not experience any major catastrophes. After all, we're adults and we know what life is about and we're not going to be misled by someone who writes a book and tries to scare us. That's certainly not my style. But I do believe that **none of us are ever going to understand what real happiness is all about if we spend the rest of our time on this earth just going through the motions.**

Ask yourself: Do you want to be a mere survivor who misses out on the real joys of successful living? Do you want to suppress that glorious quality in yourself that could let you go down any road you want at whatever speed you desire?

Do you want to let circumstances around you control your destiny—or do you want to give yourself the opportunity to control your own destiny?

You Can Control Your Destiny

MAYBE THIS WILL HELP PUT THINGS IN PERSPECTIVE. I'D like you to take a little personal survey in which you answer questions that may not seem very significant. What they are designed to do, however, is help you to see if you are happy about where you're going in your present life's journey.

This survey takes only about ten seconds. It's just two questions. And I think you'll agree it gets right to the point.

Okay, here they are. Please answer each question as sincerely as you can.

1. *If you were told you had just one year to live, would you continue to live your life the same way you are living it now?*

2. *Imagine that you are about to retire from your life's work and there is a testimonial dinner in your honor. Do you feel that the speakers that evening will be able to say the kinds of things about you that describe a woman who has become all she has dreamed of becoming?*

I believe we sometimes need to be reminded that we have a very limited time on this earth, and all any of us have are our "todays." We don't have a long time to waste. And I find it disheartening that many women will go to their graves never having experienced that feeling when you know every piston in your inner engine is churning to its fullest power, when you are absolutely certain that you're in balance with yourself and the world around you, and when you are running so smoothly that you can visualize and feel a perfect peaceful "hum" inside yourself.

To achieve this peaceful hum, *we need to learn to enjoy every single precious moment of each remaining day in joy.* So, please, stop what you are doing, take a slow, deep breath, and ask yourself what you would really *love* for your life to be like a year from now. What about five years from now? Do you want to quit your job and start a new career? Do you want to turn what is now a passionate hobby into a thriving business? Do you want a more complete home life?

And are you sure the road you are on will get you where you want to go?

A lot of us don't know how to answer these questions. Deep down, we wonder if we can make a difference in directing our own lives. We wonder if other women were born with more potential than we have. We wonder if some people—but not us—are just destined to have things go their way. We wonder why others seem to get the "breaks" in life and why we don't.

What I believe is that each one of us has the power to orchestrate our own success. The sad truth is that a lot of us subconsciously live in an environment that holds us back, keeping us on a bumpy road much too long. When we get to that point where the road diverges—one branch heading toward an exciting destination, the second to someplace comfortable or familiar—we inevitably take the latter one. It's easier to hold ourselves back than take the road less traveled.

Why? Why do we do it? Why do so many of us step away from the opportunities that come our way? Is it because we feel we should be "safe"? What about the risks we've wanted to take but refused to because we thought we didn't have the courage?

The Need to Find Ourselves

WHEN I TALK TO WOMEN, I OFTEN ASK THEM WHAT IT would take for them to be happy. I ask, "If you were financially secure, and you could live whatever sort of life you wanted, what would your life be like?"

Like most women raised in our society, these women frequently start off by talking about the great homes they'd buy, then they list the trips they would take to Europe, or to the Caribbean, or wherever.

And when I ask what they would do after they fulfill their material desires, there is often a dead silence. Many women are not sure what to say. Some of us are not in touch with what our deepest dreams are. As a result, the focus is most often on financial success. It's as if we have forgotten to entertain the idea of emotional success—a success composed of real peace and inner happiness.

I once asked a woman who had just joined our company, "Do you remember a time when you used to dream about creating a beautiful life for yourself?"

"Well," she replied, "I used to think like that."

"What did you dream about?" I asked.

The woman, whom we'll call Cheryl—and you'll be hearing a lot more about her later—stared down at her feet, deep in thought. Finally, she looked up at me. "Jinger," she said, "I've spent years just going through the same old routine without thinking about my dreams. I think I've forgotten what they are."

I guess I don't have to tell you that Cheryl is not all that unusual. Many of us have played it safe for so long—or, in some cases, allowed ourselves to be pushed down for so long—that we don't have a clue anymore what it's like to even dream. What's more, so many of us have spent so long being slightly unhappy—or, in some cases, very unhappy—that we don't know what it would take for us to become happy. Others of us have been so out of touch with our real inner selves that we haven't allowed ourselves the pleasure of dreaming.

"Jinger," women have told me, "you don't know what it's like to feel trapped. You're successful. You're well known. You run your own company. You've been married twenty-five years to a great husband. You have your children, you have no financial worries. What do you know about that indecision that haunts you when you don't have a clue what you want or how to get it?"

To that statement, I always have the same response: "Great things in life don't happen to anyone until we get the bad things in our lives out."

It's true. I couldn't appreciate my best qualities until I figured a way to get rid of my self-destructive liabilities that made me turn right when I knew I should be turning left. **I couldn't figure out what was the right road for my life until I learned what the wrong roads were.**

My Own Story

LET ME BRIEFLY GIVE YOU AN EXAMPLE OF HOW I MIStakenly tried to persuade myself that I was on the right road. This was during a period before Dick and I started our business in 1981. Even though I did have a great marriage to Dick—a sales executive who I knew was my soul mate the moment I met him—and even though I adored my children, I had a persistent, nagging feeling of dissatisfaction about what I was doing with my life. I knew I was somehow separated from some deeper feeling of inner joy and completeness. I was uncertain how to set free what I knew was my powerful feminine spirit. In sum: I didn't truly believe in myself.

Now this doesn't seem like all that big of a deal, does it? I mean, our family was financially secure, we had prosperous friends and neighbors, we went to a nice church in Dallas. . . . Hey, our life was, well, *nice.*

So why did I feel deprived in some way? Why did I lack self-confidence? Why did I believe my talents were being wasted?

I was no different from millions of other women in this country—women who have been in therapy or have sat through programs designed to "empower" them, yet who emotionally don't seem to be able to give themselves permission to let go and find their true selves.

So I did what many of us do. I decided to cover up my anxieties. I tried to look like the picture of contentment. I wore nice, chic clothes and made sure I was always vivacious. I put on an attitude when I was around others, telling them that my life was "fabulous"—one of my favorite, most overused words of that time—and that I didn't really need anything else to make me happy.

I kept thinking that if I could keep myself (and other people) oriented toward my external image, then I would not have to look at what I was like inside. So I kept making myself out to be attractive, socially desirable, and full of oh-so-interesting conversation. As long as people were paying me compliments—"Jinger, you really have it all together"—then I didn't have to face what I knew was the truth. When it came to real inner success, I felt like an impostor.

What I did not know was that I was caught in a vicious circle. To keep people from seeing beneath my packaging, I became even more fixated on my appearance, striving to stay in control, acting more and more "excited" about everything that was going on in my life. I became more and more dependent on recognition from others—whether it was prestige or honor for my accomplishments. My sense of well-being depended far more on other people than it did on myself.

Do you see what was happening? The comfort zone I had thought would get me through life was becoming my own personal prison. Despite all my preoccupation with my outward self, I became even more insecure about my identity.

And instead of getting onto the right road, I stayed exactly where I was for a tragically long period of time. I was unknowingly stuck in my false identity, locked in the same unsatisfying roles, maintaining my same old destructive habits. I diligently tried to believe that the wrong road I was traveling on was really the right one.

Little did I realize—until it was almost too late—that I was throwing away a part of myself, the part that harbored my greatest hopes and dreams.

The Fear of Our Personal Steering Wheels

WHY DID I DO THAT? WHY WOULD I NEED TO PUT ON such a "front" for other people? Why was I too intimidated to turn the steering wheel to get on the right road?

Well, that's the hard part.

The reason I wouldn't change is for the same simple reason you may be afraid to turn your own steering wheel. I was scared to believe in myself. I mean, really believe in myself. Not pretend to believe. I'm referring to the kind of belief that is so strong that if I made a wrong turn I would be capable of getting myself back on the right road.

The fact was that as confident and as exuberant as I appeared in public, I was scared deep down about stripping off my old identity and showing who I really was. Making such a decision required courage and commitment—not just "positive thinking" slogans that were easy to memorize.

I thought my life would be "good enough" if I could "look good enough," or to put it another way, act out in various false roles that I had chosen for myself. But like the demons in Pandora's box, the inner pain and unresolved conflict of my life that I tried to keep shut away kept escaping. And that is why, one day, I found myself crying so uncontrollably that I checked myself into a hospital. Remember from the Introduction how I had come to the low point of my life? This was it! I stayed an entire week. I didn't know, really, why I was crying except for the fact that I knew an essential part of myself was missing. I just wanted to get away from everyone, to run away and hide, to escape and cast off this emotional pain that I could not begin to understand.

That was the beginning for me—my first step toward the right road. Some of you have far more dramatic stories of pain and despair that form your own dark night of the soul; some of you might not have a dramatic story at all. It doesn't matter. **I believe we all have been through a period in which we have felt lost, afraid, overwhelmed, and disconnected.**

How do we stop seeing ourselves as the way we *are* and start imagining ourselves as the way we *can be?*

As I found out the hard way, before you figure out how to get on the right road in life, you've got to figure out how to get off the wrong one. And then you have to figure out why you got on the wrong road in the first place. Otherwise, even if someone gives you good directions to find the right road, you'll end up on another wrong road anyway.

The next couple of chapters are going to be interesting. We're going to take a trip into what has been called our "shadow side." We're going to find out that many women have lost touch with the best part of themselves and we're going to learn why women put on false identities in order to get through daily life. We're going to go back into our pasts to find out what messages we received that kept us from believing in ourselves. We're going to study why we have unintentionally given away bits and pieces of ourselves, gradually giving up one little part at a time to appease or please someone else.

The shadow side. Does that sound frightening? Don't let it be. I'm convinced that after you read the next couple of chapters, you'll actually feel a sense of relief. I know that you will get a better understanding of why your inner engine has been misfiring for so long. When I talk about our shadow side, I'm not talking about some evil part of us. We're simply going to look at the things inside us that make us hit the "stoplights" in our journey through life and eventually get us on the wrong road—the road to nowhere.

I truly wish all humans could afford psychoanalysis; however, since most don't have that opportunity, this is a practical book with tried-and-true advice for real women. But there's no way around it. If any of us truly want to break away from self-destructive behavior, then we have to recognize how we create it or engage in it. We have to identify the things that hold us back.

Ironically, many of us don't see how we cause harm to our own lives. We don't see how some of us are emotionally eroding away, one fragment of ourselves at a time. And many of us don't realize that as long as we stick to the old roads, we will never find out how capable we really can be. Nor will we find out how freeing it is to let go.

So here we go. As odd as this may sound, try hard to get excited about examining and confronting your shadow side. You're about to take your first steps to freeing your wondrous inner spirit, to rebuilding your engine, to truly believing in yourself.

Indeed, you're on your way to finding the part of yourself that I like to call "Positively You."

The Clogs in Your Inner Engine

What Is It That Keeps Slowing You Down?

*We can't make that first step toward the future until we let go
of the past. By just letting go of the negative messages of our
past, we have a much better chance of setting ourselves free from
our self-doubts and fears.*

PLEASE DO AN EXERCISE WITH ME. IT'S CALLED A "VISUALIZA-
tion" exercise.

One of the best ways to understand your hopes and
dreams is through visualization. It's very important for us to
sometimes visualize ourselves in the place we want to be in
the future or to see ourselves as being perfectly happy
human beings. I think our minds are sometimes like beauti-

ful, sleek dolphins you see at amusement parks that are never allowed out of their little man-made tanks. The value of visualization is that we see our dolphins swimming fast and free and playing happily in the vast blue ocean. We are going to find out things about ourselves that we never could while we kept our dolphins (our minds) in their small, familiar tanks.

In a later chapter, I'll pass on some techniques about basic, practical visualization. But, for now, all I want you to do is to try and remember a moment when you felt at your absolute best. It doesn't have to be a moment when you did something "significant." It could be when you sang a song to your child, or when you solved a complicated problem at work or school, or when you started exercising again and felt so proud and invigorated. Just remember that feeling.

Now, with that image in your mind, get ready to stop reading for a few seconds. As you think about that time when you felt your personal best, I want you to close your eyes and lock that image onto your brain (close your eyes now).

When you open your eyes and get back to this place in the book, ask yourself these questions:

Why is it we do not strive ceaselessly to have those moments in our lives as often as we can?

Why is it, when we have one of those moments, we do not diligently try to recreate such moments again?

Why do we seem not to want to relive those moments, to feel again that joy and release that come with such positive energy?

What Keeps Us from Our Dreams?

THE TRUTH IS THAT WE'RE OFTEN SAYING TO OURSELVES that we should change our lives and do what we can to reach our personal best. But in the end something stops us. Something inside us keeps us from trying. Something stops us from believing in ourselves and going for our dreams.

What is it? What keeps us from starting the new business that we've always wanted to start? What keeps us from finally deciding to get on a lifelong fitness plan? Why won't we go the extra mile to get our financial affairs in order? Why don't we do what it takes to experience loving relationships, to feel the harmony between ourselves and the world we live in, to feel the power within that will let us accomplish just about anything we set out to accomplish?

Here we are with such a thirst for change, and we're still not where we want to be—all because of this "something" that clicks off inside us right at the point at which we're about to change.

That "something" is our history. Every moment of our lives is affected by mental pictures of our own particular history. After my years of working with women, and trying to understand some of their fear at stepping forward, **I am more convinced than ever that any void in our lives goes back to our childhoods.** It's where all our feelings about ourselves began. It's where we developed our ideas about how capable we were as women, how we should act, and how we should behave.

We like to think that because our childhood is long over, we're not affected by it anymore. But it was in childhood that we first began to think we might be unworthy, unlovable, unable, insufficient, or inadequate. It was there that we first turned away from the glorious inner "spark" that could ignite our engines and send us forward to reach any destination we choose.

Right now, I can imagine some of you saying, "Oh, no, here comes one of those chapters about how we've got to blame our problems on our parents." Not so! I don't think blame helps us to go forward at all. Blame won't give us more wonderful feelings about ourselves. It doesn't help us to begin to visualize our futures positively.

We are responsible for who we are! We are responsible for our behavior! Now that doesn't mean that many of us were not hurt emotionally or even physically in our pasts. But I don't think blaming our present behavior on someone else gets us anywhere. That's nothing but an exercise in finding scapegoats instead of finding answers.

I'm also not a person who believes you can just ignore your past and say, "Don't worry, be happy!" Or: "Hey, let's just turn over a new leaf!" How can you change yourself if you don't know what it is that is causing your unhappiness? How can you find the solutions in your life unless you first diagnose the problem? If you're sick, the doctor doesn't say to you, "Here's a list of ways to be healthy." He first examines you to see how and why you think you're sick. He asks you to explain or discuss your symptoms.

And, more than likely, if a doctor could look inside your head at this very moment, he'd say, "What's really making you feel emotionally upset are lessons you learned long ago. What's sabotaging your happiness today is something you learned yesterday."

And you, in response, might reply, "What?"

"You're a wonderfully healthy person with tremendous potential," the doctor would say. "You just don't know it."

To which you might reply, "Uh, Doc, do you still have a license to practice medicine?"

Actually, the doctor is making perfect sense. Our feelings of guilt, anxiety, fear, self-pity, and lack of self-esteem all got started in childhood, and they have been repeated over and over infinite times since. We "learned" those feelings through the ways we were raised. Think about that. Our fears and anxieties were learned from long-ago, obsolete experiences—yet we are still holding on to them. We are still letting them govern our lives.

Isn't that amazing? **Most of our attitudes toward ourselves haven't changed since our formative years!**

I once heard this saying: "Life isn't the sum of what you have been. Life is what you yearn to be." It's true. But we can't make that first step toward the future, I realized, until we let go of the past. By just letting go of the negative messages of our past, we have a much better chance of setting ourselves free from our self-doubts and fears. We have to stop trying to conceal those negative messages that have been circulating in our minds for years and start confronting them head-on— messages that suggested we were not smart enough, or not talented enough, or not worthy of speaking out and sharing our feelings. We have to go back over our preadult years and examine the standards by which we have learned to judge ourselves—and also by which we have learned to *disbelieve* in ourselves. We have to understand our "history" in order to understand why we respond to situations the way we do. In truth, if we can understand what happened to us in our childhood—and understand that we can *unlearn* that belief just as we once *learned* it—we will feel so much more confident to go forward. We will realize that we are not stuck in a rut, but that we are a lot better than we believe.

Unlearning Your Past

As I said in the last chapter, I spent years of my adult life playing roles for others because I felt that being myself wasn't good enough and that being someone else would please others more. Trying always to do more or please every single person I met was exhausting. Because I was such a "people pleaser," others thought that I was a very happy person. But I felt like a fugitive because I wouldn't try to please myself. I thought there was no way I could please myself and still be liked by others at the same time.

Why was I scared about showing my true self? Why did I feel blocked about getting on the right road to achieve my hopes and dreams?

The answer is painfully simple. The childhood that I thought I had walled off—and the attitudes about myself that I had formed there—were still shaping who I was.

I had what a therapist might call an "intriguing" family background. Let me just hit some of the . . . um . . . highlights. My father (God bless him) was raised in a brothel that his stepmother operated in New Mexico, and by the time he was ten years old, he was on his own, living alone in a hotel and working there as a clerk and bellhop. When my mom was still in preschool, she was abandoned by her mother. My mother married my father when she was only fifteen years old and he was all of sixteen. My older brother was born four years later.

I spent my childhood in the West Texas towns of Amarillo and Dumas watching "perfect families" relate to one another on television. *Father Knows Best, Ozzie and Harriet, My Three Sons, Make Room for Daddy*—I knew all the episodes. The reality of my childhood life was something different. I was dyslexic. I had trouble sequencing words and numbers. At the age of thirteen, I woke up at 4:30 on summer mornings and rode in the back of a pickup truck to a field of maize—a kind of feed given to cattle. All day long, I walked up and down those rows of maize, each row two miles long, and I removed one fertile stalk after another. This process was called roguing maize. I was paid $1.35 an hour. If a rattlesnake was around, it was up to me to kill it with a shovel. If I needed to go to the bathroom, I had to squat down right there in the maize field.

I was a plain-looking child. My teeth were not only buckteeth, they also protruded and overlapped and were brown from the excess fluoride found naturally in West Texas water.

My mother was a fiercely dedicated woman, trying to keep our family afloat. She worked hard as a bookkeeper during the day, and for extra money, she saved tops from milk bottles, which she redeemed for toys to give us. She and my father had a stormy relationship. It seemed that they were separated more than they were married. My father was a handsome, charismatic salesman—he literally could sell anything, he read constantly and was very bright, but he was an alcoholic most of the years I knew him. I'm grateful that he wasn't physically abusive; he was the type who would pass out from drinking almost every night.

I always looked forward to Christmas with wild hope, as most children do. Since my birthday is on Christmas Day, you can imagine the high expectations I felt. Not only did Santa come at the same time as my own birthday, but it was the time of the year when my mother and father always got back together. To me, Christmas was the season when we would be a real family. Every Christmas as a child, I hoped and prayed that, this time, my parents finally would stay together.

But not soon afterward, my father would be gone again, and my mother would be working day and night, and my brother and I would be alone. At the beginning of third grade, when I was just eight years old, I cried every day for four and a half weeks. Little did anyone know that I was really depressed, unable to get a hold of what was happening around me. In Amarillo, Texas, at that time, people did not visit child therapists. Plus, we couldn't have afforded it anyway. The school nurse didn't know what to do with me. She'd let me lie on the daybed in her office and just cry. Eventually, she stopped calling my mother each day at work, because there was nothing my mother could do, either, and she would lose her job if she came to school anymore.

My mother did what she could to keep our family together. Throughout my childhood she would divorce and remarry my father. During one period when they were divorced, Mom married my stepfather. When I was fifteen, my mother decided she had to get away from him, too, so we packed everything we could get into a car, and we drove to Michigan, where my father was living. Three weeks later, my mother and my stepfather reconciled, and we came back to Texas.

I finished the rest of that school year in Texas. At the end of school, we again packed up the car and moved to Michigan, where I finished my high school years and went to college.

Because of both my parents' problems—my dad being "absent" either emotionally or physically, and my mother always working two jobs—I often felt completely alone, as well as unloved, unattractive, and unacknowledged.

It would be easy to read my story and say that nothing was my fault—that I should have seen what was happening around me and realized it had nothing to do with my own self-esteem. But, like most children, I internalized my family problems. I thought it was my fault in some way that things weren't smooth. I surmised I was not lovable and unconsciously decided that what I had to do to get love was to be noticed.

So, I learned how to move into a position where I became the center of attention, for however brief a time. I learned to talk without pause—lest I be ignored or interrupted. I learned to "look" good. I got my teeth fixed. I learned to smile demurely. I learned to hide my weight around the middle. I learned how to make persuasive eye contact by staring at a person's right eye when talking to him or her, which helps you "make the sale." (Try it, it works.)

By the time I got to high school, I was focused on achievement. I received an A+ in the hardest literature course at school, I was named to the homecoming court, I became editor of the yearbook, and I won the school's best-dressed award. I am blessed with a mother who sews beautifully and taught me to sew. We would go shopping in a nice department store but couldn't afford the clothes. My mother would trace a pattern from a dress that fit me. Then we would leave the store and go buy fabric to make a similar dress.

Today, I'm very proud of my ability to stand up and express myself persuasively in front of others. I like looking my best in front of others. But back then, instead of celebrating those qualities about myself, I was desperately using them to cover up my feelings of inadequacy. I tried to appeal to others in the best light possible—doing everything I could to conceal the evidence that my light wasn't all that bright in the first place. To compensate for my childhood feelings that I was unworthy, I started playing "roles."

I became the school's human *doing* instead of human *being*. Besides all my extracurricular activities, I excelled as a salesperson at an exclusive shoe store, and I never, ever missed a day of work. I hated not being busy, and subconsciously I hated being alone. If I was, there was the chance that those old feelings of not being heard would come back—feelings of being unloved. So if I ever found myself alone, I would find something to work on. Cleaning and organizing, for example, became major projects. I worked for praise and compliments.

Indeed, once I started getting a little praise and attention, it was like my drug of choice. Being heard was my need—the void inside me that needed to be filled! As long as I was doing something—as long as I was getting recognition for what I was doing—I naïvely believed that I was covering up my lack of self-esteem. To put it another way, I thought I had figured out a way not to hit the curbs in life by learning to aim the steering wheel slightly to the left. I made some adjustments—but I didn't solve the problem!

Amazing, isn't it? For so long, I was able to hold on to an old mental image about myself that I had learned from my distant childhood. I still carried with me so many childhood feelings of worthlessness and inadequacy long after I had "proved" that I was different.

I refused to let go of something that was then. And, not surprisingly, I was unable to live in the now.

And you know what? I couldn't hide it forever. As competent as I appeared on the outside, my emotions were like a stewpot beginning to boil over. There was no way for the lid to stay in place. I would lapse into depression and crying spells. And during all that time, what I never realized was that my attempts to avoid anxiety were only creating greater anxiety.

By letting go of painful past attitudes—attitudes that were never of our creation—we can look at ourselves in a different way and come alive again. It's really like a whole new lease on life. We must look into the past precisely in order to make some changes in our future. Only with the insight of knowing how we arrived at our present road in life can we take measures to change our direction. This insight is the key to becoming "Positively You!"

Our Hidden Negative Messages

A BOUT NOW, YOU MAY BE SAYING, "WAIT A SECOND, Jinger. I don't know if I can relate to any of this. I had a *happy* childhood."

This point is well-taken. Many of us did have happy childhoods. (My own childhood was filled with moments of terrific happiness.) Others of us grew up in perfectly uneventful ways, with parents who did the best they could to help us. A few of us grew up with model parents whom we spend most of our lives trying to emulate.

But even if you had those kinds of parents, let me ask this question: **Are you still afraid to totally believe in yourself?**

I'm not someone who thinks we all had some sort of "hidden" childhood abuse that we have repressed into our subconscious so that we no longer remember it. But what we have to recognize is that the past is like a great memory bank: it is filled with lots of wonderful and positive messages, and it also is filled with messages that may have made us discouraged about ourselves or others.

Whether we realize it or not, almost all of us received some sort of negative messages that have had a residual effect. I know a woman who is one of the most intelligent people I have ever met. Yet she holds herself back. She doesn't express her intelligence to others, and she seems uncomfortable when she is put on the spot and asked to give an opinion. I didn't understand her until one day when she told me that her brothers had resented her in childhood for being so smart. She recalled that her teachers seemed more irritated than pleased that she didn't seem to work hard in school yet knew all the answers. She started hiding her intelligence.

Now, my friend didn't make a conscious decision to be "unsmart." But after a few years, she began connecting being smart with being unlovable. She began to have trouble concentrating in school. Her grades tumbled. And she didn't do anything about it. Although she didn't know it, she un-consciously had decided to submerge or even sabotage her talents.

Let me give you another example that almost all of us as women can identify with. Somewhere in our childhood was the message that failure is the dreaded enemy. We were taught by the people who surrounded us that it was wrong to fail. This was not a malicious lesson, of course. But many of us began to learn to create a life for ourselves based on that mes-sage. Instead of really going for what we wanted, we created a safer life—a "safety zone." To use one of my automobile analogies, we adamantly stayed on the far right lane on a highway, refusing to get up to even the minimum speed limit. We made a lot of "safe" decisions and formed a lot of self-protective beliefs that reinforced the fact that we shouldn't do this or that in order to avoid the *possibility of failure.*

The problem was that the more we lived in that safety zone, the more afraid we became of trying to do something more with ourselves. We knew the safety zone wasn't very enriching. In fact, it produced more anxiety than comfort because we were not striving for a better life. Nevertheless, the longer we were in that zone, the more we lost our courage. We started restricting our world and skewing our behavior in order to avoid situations that might threaten our safety.

Do you remember Cheryl, the woman I was telling you about earlier? She was the one who told me she had spent years on autopilot, going through her routine, not thinking about her dreams. If you had met her, you would have thought she was listless. She didn't have enthusiasm for anything.

Well, when we started talking, I asked about her growing-up years. She told me her parents were wonderful because they were very protective of her.

"What do you mean?" I asked.

"They were real concerned about who I made friends with, what new activities I tried. They were always telling me about being safe, about being careful. They wanted me to know just how dangerous the world was."

That doesn't seem to be a negative message at all, does it? But as Cheryl kept talking, I realized that she had interpreted that message in a different way. Her parents, she also told me, had lived in the same house all their lives. Her father had stayed in the same job, and her mother rarely left the house except to go to church or to the grocery store. Cheryl's parents never argued. In a way, everything they did was to control their environment, away from the outside world. They had set up their lives to protect themselves from life.

As she got older, that attitude stayed inside Cheryl's head, and as an adult, she became afraid to try anything new or different for herself.

It's All of the Little Messages

BECAUSE SO MUCH WRITING AND ATTENTION OVER THE last few years has been devoted to "dysfunctional families," many of us have come to think that if we escaped terribly traumatic or abusive situations at home, then we should have no problems. That, too, is a mistake. I believe it's not the one or two traumatic events in a person's life that are significant, but rather the constant, seemingly insignificant messages we may not always remember. It's those little messages that we received over and over that led us to develop certain beliefs about our world, about other people, and about ourselves.

Ultimately, because of these messages, we often send the best and most creative sides of ourselves underground. We start acting more on the assumption that we are inadequate rather than terrific. These assumptions become self-fulfilling, so that by the time we are adults, our belief in our inadequacy has been reinforced many times over.

And what happens if we do not change? We get caught in a swirling cycle in which our lives are nothing more than a reenactment of our pasts. Psychologists will tell us that we have a fundamental tendency as human beings to repeat our past experiences. We will find ourselves unconsciously orchestrating things that happen to us to fit those old attitudes taught to us by our pasts. We will use emotions of the past to deal with people in the present. We will react to life with certain emotions because that is how we have been trained. When a bright little girl, for example, is called "stupid" enough times by bigger people, she'll eventually start going along and acting stupid just to fit in with the script she thinks she must follow. Years later, when that bright little girl is a grown woman, she will face every challenge with the feeling that maybe she is too stupid to succeed.

If we learn what made us the way we are, then we have the chance to take a journey into the future that is full of excitement, of joy, and of true inner peace. Perhaps this illustration will help. Have you ever walked into a movie after the first third of it has already been shown? You spend the rest

of the movie wondering what is going on. Even if you figure out what the plot is, you still know you are missing
some of the crucial details that will help you piece it all together.

So it is with our lives. A lot of us have missed the first
third of our own movie—our childhoods. We've neglected
to piece together some understanding of what happened
there. We haven't figured out what the meaning is of the
messages we received from significant others. As a result, we
can be doomed to repeat our self-destructive actions—and
without reviewing the past, we're not going to be able to do
much about the future.

Now let's take a closer look at how our pasts are still af-
fecting the way we direct our lives.

Grabbing Hold of the Wheel

Why Are You Afraid to Take Charge of Your Life?

Millions of us never recognize that we work very hard at
avoiding happiness. We think we have figured out a way to
suppress what we believe are our negative qualities. But what we
really are doing is losing touch with our greatest capabilities.

I WILL BE THE FIRST TO ADMIT THAT IT'S NOT EASY TO GO BACK over our preadult years and examine the "messages" by which we learned to judge ourselves. Think about how you sleep. Don't you almost always sleep in the same comfortable, familiar position? Now think about going to sleep in a different position. Doesn't the mere idea make you feel uncomfortable? Imagine the discomfort of having to lie that way all night.

If changing a simple body position is that hard, think of what it's going to be like to change an emotional position you have held about yourself for your entire adulthood!

As you're going to find out in the second half of this book, the changes will come. **Like a wound that has been covered and allowed to fester, our inner selves will heal a good deal faster if we can bring our pasts into the open, examine them, fix them, and then break away from them forever!** Tracking down the negative messages of our childhoods—and then figuring out the "roles" we play to deal with those messages—is the first major challenge in creating a new self-image.

Reconnecting to Our Strengths

THERE'S NOTHING WRONG WITH ADOPTING DIFFERENT roles in life. Just as we wear different clothes for different occasions, it's sometimes wise to show various shades of ourselves in order to live more effectively in society.

But the challenge comes when we spend more time acting in our "roles" rather than rebuilding our self-esteem. We turn to roles instead of turning to true self-examination to find out who we really are, what we really want, and what we are truly capable of becoming. Although we think these "roles" make us look as if we're coping more successfully with life, what eventually happens is that they often lead us to even greater unhappiness. Because I was trying so hard to be noticed—because I so needed strokes from others—I began to lose touch with my real strengths. I was unable to recognize my best qualities, which those people whom I was trying to impress would have genuinely appreciated.

My overreactions to life were signs that something was the matter. Instead of looking for the right road for my life, I was almost obsessively remaining on the wrong road, trying to fill a void from childhood. Like a magnet, the past was still drawing me into my old roles. Saddest of all, I was missing out on those beautiful, wonderful moments that could have been an everyday part of my life. My roles created a prison that kept me confined. They kept me from my essence—from my best self.

To refuse to understand the past and then let it go is to ensure that you will remain forever imprisoned. I know that sounds harsh, but it happens. Janice was a woman I knew who automatically smiled and nodded her head encouragingly when people talked to her. After I met her, I found myself admiring her ability to be so agreeable. She never seemed to get annoyed with anyone, and she almost never disagreed with anything anyone said. When I once asked Janice how she was able to stay so sweet throughout all the headaches that life brings, she told me that she lived by the age-old adage "If you can't say something nice, don't say anything at all."

A couple of years later, I saw Janice again. This time, she was a much different woman. She didn't put on her beauty-pageant smile, and she didn't try to act overjoyed. When I asked her if anything had changed, she told me that she and her husband were separating.

"Not you two!" I said.

"He told me he could no longer handle my anger," the woman said in a resigned voice.

"Anger?" I said. "You were *angry?* I've never even heard an angry tone in your voice."

"Jinger," she replied, "you wouldn't believe the kinds of tantrums I have thrown over little things."

I was so startled I hardly knew what to say.

"Do you know why I tried to be so kind all the time?" Janice told me. "It was because I was afraid of my own anger. I thought anger was wrong. So outside the house, I would just stuff it. I thought it would be unflattering if people saw that in me. But when something happened at home, I'd dump all my anger on my family. I unloaded on my children as well as my husband."

Janice went on to say that she wasn't sure what was going wrong until she began to talk with her sister and a psychologist about her childhood. "I remembered that my mother and father were always bickering. They didn't get into big shouting matches often—but when they did, watch out! My father was terrifying. I thought when he got really angry he might do something violent."

Anger is a natural emotion—as natural as breathing—yet many of us women have never known how to deal with it. To avoid the anger she saw in her parents—and to avoid the anger she knew was in her as well—Janice created a role for herself. She put on a "nice" act in hope we would all admire her, which we did. But the role was never enough. As Janice later told me, her role was giving her severe headaches. Away from us, when everyday situations would arise at home, the anger that emerged in her was way out of proportion to the situation. "It was awful," she told me. "I would become provoked at the slightest incident—and I ended up falling apart."

Today, I'm happy to say that Janice has broken free of her role and reunited with her family. "I have found that I can express my anger appropriately without losing control and being a 'bad' person," she said. "And what's even more amazing is that people appreciate me more because I don't act so perfect. I'm more fun to be with because I'm relaxed and more myself. I just wish it hadn't taken a crisis like a near divorce to teach me to learn what I was doing to myself."

Do You Unconsciously Try to Avoid Happiness?

A S YOU CAN SEE, JANICE STARTED OUT IN HER "ROLE" FOR all the right reasons. There was nothing wrong with her being nice. But she mistakenly thought that by being extra-nice, she could ignore the emotionally distorted messages of her past.

Fortunately, Janice did what we all eventually have to do: she identified her role. Just by doing that, she had taken the first step in getting her engine started and turning the steering wheel toward the right road.

Millions of us never recognize that we work very hard at avoiding happiness. We think we have figured out a way to suppress what we believe are our negative qualities. But what we really are doing is losing touch with our greatest capabilities. And as the years go on, we do not know what it takes to believe in that self again.

We are so used to being in our roles—hiding behind our masks—that we have trouble imagining what life would be like with those masks off. Few women get to the point of understanding that the real joy in life comes when we discard our roles—the very things that we think we need to cope.

Learning to start over and "find" our true selves is not a simple task, nor one that comes easily to us. We have spent our lifetimes learning to adapt to others' expectations of us. Many of us have spent our lifetimes perfecting our psychological defense mechanisms, convinced that life will be satisfying only if we hide our feelings and bury them beneath layers of social skills.

And, so, we drift farther and farther away from expressing our real selves in everyday life. We not only become alienated from the world we live in and alienated from those we love, but we also become alienated from our own potential as human beings. We lose ourselves. We give bits of ourselves away by denying our true feelings. **Many of us poison our potential as human beings.**

But enough of this doom and gloom. Like my friend Janice, we can change our behavior. We don't have to act as if the past were in the present or as if the people of the past still had power to shape our current behavior. One woman I knew constantly downplayed her relationships with her friends. When calling one of us, she would say in a monotone, "I guess you don't recognize who this is, do you?" When she told a story, she doubted herself. She'd say, "You're probably not interested in this, but . . ." Even though we'd assure her we were very interested in what she was saying, she would reply, "Oh, you're just saying that to make me feel better."

In her own way, this woman had created a distinct "role" for herself as a victim. It was a role that would lead to rejection from others. Who, after all, would want to spend a lot of time around such a negative person? It was so exhausting trying to reassure her or "care" for her. Too much work was required to be her friend. I call people like her high maintenance.

This woman played the victim role so well that she became one! Possibly, in her past, she had been a victim in some way, so to let go of this behavior was very difficult for her. After all, her safety zone was to play this role. It was more normal for her to be reassured by others that she was interesting and worthwhile than it was for her to look into her past and ask herself what made her think she wasn't interesting and worthwhile.

Today, that woman (I'm not mentioning her name to protect her privacy) is one of our company's most successful

Sales Directors. She makes a great salary, she is naturally poised and relaxed, she walks forward joyfully to shake your hand, and she loves to share with you her attitude toward life. She can give a fabulous motivational speech, describing how the mind is immeasurable, capable of accomplishing anything it focuses on. Most of all, her friends like me are ecstatic when we hear from her. She is so full of positive energy that it cannot help but seep into our own lives as well.

How did she do it? "I got rid of the baggage," she likes to say. "I realized that I was still stuck in a period in my childhood when I felt as if I was destined for constant rejection. I had to teach myself that no matter what happened in my past, it didn't have to impact the person I am today."

In other words, although she might have had every past reason to believe she was a victim, she decided she had no present reason to believe it. "I realized I could be responsible for my own happiness," she told me. "As simple as that sounds, it is a powerful feeling."

Liking yourself and being happy is an active choice! You just have to decide you want it. "It's not the events of our lives that shape us, but our beliefs as to what those events mean," motivational author Anthony Robbins has written. "We need to remember that most of our beliefs are generalizations about our past." Indeed, all we have to do is tell ourselves that we don't have to live with the "interpretation" we have put on our pasts. We don't have to live with those negative feelings about ourselves that are nothing more than learned responses from childhood.

We can cast off the myth that was part of our childhood development, and we can be directed by our inner voice rather than the cacophony of outer voices that dominated our histories. We can find our own paths to successful living. **We can manage our destinies!**

And what a relief it is to just be ourselves. I will never forget a story I once heard about a woman named Gloria, who had accumulated a string of unsuccessful romantic relationships. The guys she met showed some initial interest in her, but eventually they moved on. Gloria had resigned herself to a life of loneliness.

It so happened, however, that Gloria's best friend had to leave town on a work assignment for several months, and she asked Gloria to visit her brother occasionally and make sure he was all right. Gloria did so, and the man fell head over heels for her.

What happened? Because of her poor sense of self, Gloria had been putting on an artificial façade to impress the men she was meeting, thinking that they would never be interested in her if they saw the "real" Gloria. But the façade was so false that it sent guys running. Only with her friend's brother, when she relaxed and acted like herself, did she discover the truth. She discovered she was really likable without having to resort to some false and superficial role.

Bombarded by Self-Doubt

I SUSPECT YOU MAY BE WONDERING IF I'M GOING TO SUGGEST that you are going to need years of professional therapy to understand what happened to you long ago. I believe therapy can help everyone. And if you can afford it and choose to pursue that avenue, great! It's a structured way for you to hold up a mirror to your inner self and figure out what's there. Should that be your desire, then I would recommend that you be relentless in finding excellent, highly recommended counselors before you begin an extended therapy program.

But I haven't written this book to send you into therapy. In fact, I know a lot of us can use therapy as a crutch to avoid taking action. We become so fascinated with studying our-selves—trying to find that one "aha" moment in our past that explains who we are—that we forget about driving for-ward down our road in life.

Besides, I don't think that you can tell exactly what type of person you have turned out to be simply by figuring out the way your parents were or how they reacted to you. Our rela-tionships with our family are not that easy to explain. For example, if your parents were plagued by financial failure throughout their lives, then you might either (a) become so determined to make it financially that you lose your ability to enjoy your inner self, or (b) feel so guilty about outshin-ing your parents that you never try to become a financial success yourself. Two different responses to the same situa-tion.

If you were a child who got a lot of approval from your parents, you might have been blessed with great self-esteem. Or you might have begun to feel like the family hero and thus felt timid about doing anything to upset your parents or make them disappointed in you. As a result, you may have spent your life making sure you have won their approval in-stead of passionately pursuing your dreams and expressing who you really are.

Or if your parents had great expectations of you, you might have worked hard to fulfill their expectations. On the other hand, you might have decided that the only way to break from your parents was to rebel and deliberately fail, believing that you would be more comfortable with failure than success.

What if your parents were the type of people who were al-ways there to help rescue you from tough spots? You might grow up always expecting someone to come forward and rescue you again. Or because you've been helped so often, you might subconsciously believe you're not capable of "fixing" your own problems along life's road.

Do you see where we're going? Each of us responds differently to the same environment. Specifically, if you talk with your siblings about their experience, it's usually different from yours. One child from a seemingly perfect family can end up an irresponsible citizen and another from the same family can turn out to be a great success. Why? We don't really know. We can only analyze our parents and our history to a certain extent, and then we must consciously choose to go forward.

Furthermore, we as women do not need years of therapy to come to the conclusion that we have been bombarded by self-doubt. It's not someone's fault it happened. And I'm not saying that we should try to find someone to blame. It just happened! And it happens in model families, too. I've known women who felt like failures all their adult lives because they thought they could not measure up to their perfect parents. They felt that they were always falling short of the mark. The problem was they defined success by what their core family had chosen as success. They defined themselves by who their family was or what it had achieved, rather than celebrating their own lives as individuals. As a result, they turned out to be their own worst critics, driving themselves relentlessly to produce and perform in order to gain the approval they always wanted.

Frankly, there aren't many of us who got to experience the perfect family. Some of us grew up in family environments that were negative, distorted by put-downs, sarcasm, or even cruel punishment. Some of us grew up in family environments in which our parents pushed their own ideas and dreams on us instead of encouraging us to find our own vision. Some of us had parents who never tried very hard to be successful; we have either not had the courage to try hard either, or we've tried so hard that we've nearly "killed" ourselves by overheating our motors until they burned out!

Some of us were raised with mothers who were depressed, who felt unfulfilled in their lives and who didn't have the opportunities that we have had to do something for themselves. I have felt guilty at the idea of bursting forth in my own life because my own mother had to struggle so very hard. And there are those of us who have older brothers and sisters whom we desperately wanted to emulate. Yet we could never "be like them." Maybe we felt slower, smaller, clumsier, less intelligent, or less athletic. So many of us have felt as if we were puttering used cars—just not quite good enough to be compared with a shiny new luxury car.

And if that's not enough, we inherited many "shoulds" from childhood—regardless of what type of family we grew up in. The should list is endless: what kind of morals we should have, what kind of vocation is acceptable, what type of personality we should have, how we should act on our jobs, how we should spend money, how we should save it, and so on. Although so many conditions in our lives have changed, those childhood "shoulds" continue to speak inside us, guiding and controlling the decisions that we make.

What is the result of all this unconscious "learning"? **Many of us have sacrificed the possibility of achievement, wealth, fame, and happiness—all because of the idea that we aren't as capable as other people, or because we think we "should" be doing something different from what we want to do.** We remain attached to old patterns. And because many of us were not taught how to celebrate our uniqueness or to nurture ourselves, we early on began assuming "roles" to protect ourselves from rejection. I say, "Stop shoulding on yourself."

If we can recognize how our attitudes of the past have developed our roles of today, we are well on our way to un-clogging our engines and living a healthy life. The root cause of our problems in life is the schism we have set up between the best parts of ourselves that we privately sub-merge and the roles we publicly display. If we can just let our true selves come out—**if we can again learn to believe in the power of our true selves**—then we will never again be paralyzed by those feelings that we are somehow incapable. We will not lose our enthusiasm for living. We will not lose that energy for getting up and living in a fresh and vigorous way every day!

The Power of Roles

I AM GOING TO LIST SOME OF THE MORE WELL-documented roles that we play as women. As you read them, I want you to notice how many *good* qualities there are in these roles. You will see descriptions of women who are driven to excellence, and you will see women who are blessed with compassion. But what they have often done in their roles is to distort these wonderful qualities and use them as self-protective shields.

You'll probably see yourself in more than one role. Believe me, I see parts of myself in nearly all of these roles. Both my strengths and liabilities helped create those roles. By identi-fying the roles I have chosen to play, I have also been able to identify positive traits along with the negative ones. With that knowledge, I hope I am able to use the positive traits from my various roles to enhance my life while at the same time getting rid of my negative ones. For example, instead of acting overly enthusiastic as a way to hide my lack of self-esteem, I've learned to use my natural enthusiasm to moti-vate others to achieve their dreams. Instead of acting overly relentless and trying to control everything in business negotiations, I've attempted to channel my high energy, learning to be more diplomatic, empowering others, while remaining committed to my own vision.

Yes, I have been described in one national magazine as being like a wound-up Barbie doll (gee, thanks), and another magazine has said that I am the type of person who can talk "a mile a minute" (oh, even greater thanks). But you know what? I now know I'm using these characteristics to their fullest. I know I'm putting my personality to its best use. I'm working at motivating others to achieve their dreams—and in the process I've been achieving my own dreams. How can anyone complain about that?

So, figure out if you see yourself in any of these roles. And, as you do, recognize that you have glorious attributes that are just waiting to be put to their best use!

THE PERFECTIONIST: Have you ever met someone who is difficult to please no matter what she has accomplished? She has difficulty congratulating herself. She is preoccupied by what she "should" be doing and forgets to ask what she "wants" or needs. She loses touch with the spontaneous little girl inside her. Often it's hard for her to play or do something that could bring her joy.

A Perfectionist is not wrong or right, she just is. She is the person at work who delivers outstanding products and services. She is a great leader as long as she doesn't set standards that no one could ever reach. She puts tremendous pressure on herself and sometimes on others.

The Perfectionist has a need for order and routine and there is an inner pressure to use every minute productively. As a result, she is at times unable to relax, enjoy life, or easily accept what comes her way.

What happened to make her feel this way? After all, don't

we want to strive to do more and do it better? Yes, we do, but her messages from the past tell her that she wasn't good enough. Now she's trying to prove through her perfection that she's not only good enough, but that she's the best.

If women who are Perfectionists take that same passion they have for perfection and channel it into a more relaxed human-being approach, they become extraordinary leaders. The key is to relax and realize that there always is a reasonable *degree* of what is acceptable. If she's able to do that, she's not only happier, but she's nurturing herself because she's identifying her own humanness.

THE CAGED SPIRIT: This is a woman who possesses the great qualities of humility and humbleness—the very things that a lot of us could use. The problem is she hasn't developed enough courage to stand up for herself. She has yet to develop the inner strength to truly believe her opinions are important. People tend to walk over her or use her. As a result, she may bury her own desires and hopes for the future. And, as time goes on, she may become more self-conscious and vulnerable, causing her to remain inside the small space of her cage, where she feels safe.

What message do you think she received somewhere in her history? Probably that she was not enough! That's the same message the Perfectionist received, yet they each respond to that message differently. The key to the roles we play is to first understand what message we received as children and how we have responded to that message. Then, identify the role we have chosen in trying to prove the message right or wrong. The Perfectionist is trying to prove that she's *more* and doing it better than anyone. The Caged Spirit is trying to prove that she's *enough* by never rocking the boat and staying out of everyone's way. The Perfectionist is trying to prove the message of "not enough" was *wrong*. The Caged Spirit is trying to prove the message "not enough" was *right*.

THE SAINT: The Saint is always accommodating others. Indeed, recognizing that it is so important to give and serve others, the Saint has created a life for herself in which her own needs are defined by what she does for others. Unfortunately, she defines herself only through how others define her. She wants to be everyone's best friend and she's all too often disappointed when this is an unattainable goal. The Saint believes that she is somehow responsible if another person doesn't like her.

To her credit, the Saint is often a great listener, she's compassionate and cares about others' needs. She above all really desires the best for others.

What was the message she received? That she probably wasn't worth much if she didn't give of herself (this is another way of saying "not enough"). By constantly giving to others and putting her own needs and desires aside, she is trying to prove that message wrong.

THE PERFORMER: This is the woman who cannot imagine being loved just for who she is. She thinks she must be loved for her achievements or by entertaining those around her. This person is fun to be around because she keeps things lively. Sometimes the Performer focuses her attention on earning the kind of status that will guarantee others' admiration. And she's good at it. She comes across to others so well that she is respected by most everyone she meets. She is likely to be a high achiever who can present an appearance of optimism and well-being.

The Performer is not good or bad, just like all the roles.

After all, each role is chosen subconsciously as a way of proving messages right or wrong. There is no greater feeling than having achieved a goal, but depending primarily on achievement for her happiness may backfire on the Performer.

Her message would be: Perform, or fail to be acknowledged. The Performer feels somehow responsible for "carrying" the dinner party or just making people laugh. Most of us need more of a sense of humor and the ability to have fun and be witty. But the Performer believes she is loved because of her performance and not just because of who she is.

THE PRETTY WOMAN: Regardless of her talents, regardless of her intelligence, she seems obsessed with her physical appearance. To her, physical beauty is life itself. Her self-worth is dependent on how she looks. I know as a female and from working with women that we want to be attractive, and society expects us to be; yet we women often believe we fall short because we compare ourselves to un-realistic standards. Most often, women are able to be human beings first, women second, and attractive people third. Not the Pretty Woman—she finds it difficult to relax about her grooming routine. She seldom allows herself to run errands unless she has on full makeup. This is so stressful and nonnurturing to one's self. For the Pretty Woman, graduation is going without your makeup sometimes and never apologizing for how you look.

The Pretty Woman is usually one we admire because she appears to be in control since she is always pulled together. But, as pretty as she may be, she is often focused on her flaws and not on her attributes. What message do you think she received? "Not enough." She received the message that for women to be loved and accepted they have to be pretty. In other words, you're "not enough" if you're not pretty.

THE CRISIS QUEEN: This is a woman who "can't get no satisfaction." On top of that, she usually doesn't want any. Crisis and conflict make her feel normal. She probably experienced a lot of conflict in her childhood, so peace and harmony actually feel less normal than crisis.

The Crisis Queen is usually looking for a crisis, and if there's none, she will create one. One thing I have learned about crisis and conflict is that they both bring attention your way! And, interestingly enough, we as humans will sometimes create conflict to bring others closer to us. Think about it—the squeaky wheel gets the grease! In a subconscious way, when we don't know how to ask for what we need, we will create conflict—just like a child who loves getting negative attention rather than no attention at all.

All of us play this role from time to time, but if you think you might be playing Crisis Queen more often than you'd like, ask yourself what you get out of this behavior and whether there is a better way to get your needs fulfilled.

THE BLAMER: This is a woman who can go through each day of her life figuring out a new way in which she isn't appreciated. Her emotional life basically consists of complaints about her own misfortunes. She keeps herself a victim.

For the Blamer, it's far easier to groan about her condition than it is to change it. She always has an excuse for why she can't change. She has a tendency to blame everything or everyone for her circumstances.

I find it fascinating that people with physical handicaps are not usually Blamers. They are grateful for what they have rather than focusing on what they don't have.

All of us can be Blamers from time to time, but constantly looking outside ourselves to hand off responsibility will truly scar us and lead to a lonely, unhappy life.

What message do you think the Blamer received? I would guess she witnessed an important person in her life not taking responsibility for his or her own problems. Maybe she saw her mother blame her father for their problems. Whatever happened, she found that it was easier to complain about a problem than it was to take action to fix it. Plus, by acting so tragically put-upon, she could portray herself as a martyr. But remember—happiness is an *active choice!* And, as Abe Lincoln put it, "We're all just about as happy as we make up our minds to be."

THE COMPETITOR: Whatever someone is doing well, the Competitor wants to do better. She is great at taking risks and trying new things, but she has difficulty enjoying her own success. She's usually comparing herself with someone else. She has difficulty celebrating the success of others because she feels inadequate. On the other hand, the Competitor often finds success in her activities, and when channeled, her drive and ambition set new heights for all of us to reach!

It's hard to relax with the Competitor around because she makes almost everything a contest—to be won or lost. She has difficulty enjoying "the game" because she is so determined to do it better or win next time that she has a hard time staying in the present.

What was the message she received? To be valued, you must be the best. While all of us can enjoy competition, we can also enjoy the process and let go of the outcome. Being present to enjoy the actual "game" and not just be consumed with the outcome is an important message for the Competitor.

THE PROCRASTINATOR: The Procrastinator is a woman who talks about what she's going to do, but delays taking the action to achieve what she's talking about. As wonderful as it is to get all the information up front, there's a point at which we must stop talking and take action.

Usually, procrastination is about fear or fear of failure. You see, I can talk about something I want to accomplish, but if I don't do it, I can't fail! If the Procrastinator can channel her need for information by making a list of the pros and cons, and then take action, she will win! Procrastinators need to make a commitment to self that they will write out a plan with deadlines. Even if some of the deadlines aren't met, they will realize that it's not failure and they can continue on to the next step.

What do you think the Procrastinator's message was? I think the message was *Don't fail* and that mistakes are failures. The Procrastinator's other message may have been: you're "not enough" if you make mistakes, and the easy way to prevent that is to avoid action.

THE BUSY DOING: She's the woman who keeps herself so busy that she doesn't have to feel or think about her own desires or needs. Also, by having so much on her plate, she never has to truly develop one great quality in herself. Her preoccupation with "doing," for example, prevents her from showing her most creative side. She unfortunately disappoints the people she most wants to please because she usually has taken on more than any human can deliver. On the other hand, a better-balanced Busy Doing woman has what it takes to accept a challenge and get the job done.

As busy women, we can often take on too much. I believe that any woman can do anything she desires, but not all at the same time. The message the Busy Doing received was that her value was related to doing and doing more. Or, you guessed it, "not enough."

THE MUST BE: We all know this woman, don't we? This is a woman who must be right. She is uncomfortable if someone is telling a shared experience and they mention a detail that she thinks is incorrect. She will interrupt the conversation and make the correction. It's like when my hubby would share a story about us with friends and he would say, "About nine years ago." And I would interrupt and say, "No, honey, it was nine and a half years ago." Well, it didn't matter if it was nine or nine and a half. That particular detail had no bearing on the story at all. So I learned from Dr. Wayne Dyer "to think about being kind rather than right." That has helped me so much!

Our Must Be friend's message was that being right made you valuable. She must have learned that to be wrong is failure or that correcting minor details makes you somehow more important or valuable. Or maybe she learned she "wasn't enough" if she wasn't perfect.

Moving from Stress to Serenity

AFTER READING ABOUT THESE ROLES, YOU MAY FEEL YOU fit into one or more of them. Besides my Perfectionist, Performer, and Must Be roles, I have found myself being most of the above at one time or another. Remember that these roles aren't good or bad in moderation, they are simply roles that we as women will want to understand.

When I finally was able to see the roles I had chosen to play, I was able to see how I had gotten on the wrong road.

Your direction will be clear for you if you recognize the roles you have chosen for yourself and why. We can turn away from self-defeating roles and become self-nourishing instead. We can enjoy ourselves and others more than we ever dreamed possible, and, in the process, we can discover our most loving nature.

So if our past roles have been tools we have used to help us get what we needed, then why do we want to shed them? Simply because there's an easier way. We can ask for what we need and desire without assuming a role. We can grow to understand and fully believe that we are not only *enough*, but we're more than enough and have been created perfect by God just the way we really are. We can relax about being right because right isn't our self-worth. We can enjoy others' success because we love to share in happiness. We can truly want the best for others and ourselves and not give up one to have the other.

So congratulate yourself. We've made the first big step toward change. We're putting our past behind us. We're getting rid of those out-of-date tools or "roles" we used in our past. Our inner engines are unclogged and we're ready to move on.

P A R T

From Self-Doubt to Self-Confidence

Overhauling Your Life

Deep inside us, there is a voice crying out. It is a voice that is soothing and startlingly powerful. It is a voice that can change our life. What is it? It is the voice of our true self.

Start Your Engines!

Facing Your Old Fears About Change

Yes, fear of change is real. Fear is a powerful force that prevents
many of us from getting what we want from life. But the great
news is that no one is born with confidence. It's all
acquired and developed.

SO FAR, WE'VE SPENT A LOT OF TIME FIGURING OUT ALL THE
things that have held us back from accomplishing our
dreams. We've pondered why we don't always feel capable as
women. We've realized many of us have stopped believing in
ourselves. We've learned about the negative messages in the
past. We've discovered how we have taken on self-sabotaging
"roles" as a way to get by in life.

All of which lead us to ask one very simple question: *Now what do we do?*

That's what these next few chapters are about. We're going to come up with strategies for escaping from our negative world that has held us back too long. We're going to go through some simple, practical, time-tested techniques that thousands of successful people have already used to convert their self-doubt into self-confidence. Remember, winners in life are developed, not born. Just as they developed negative behaviors, they were later able to develop winning behaviors—traits that we, too, can develop in our own lives. Our winning personalities can be developed just as muscles are developed. With the right attitude and exercises, and with the commitment to perform these exercises, we will see dramatic results.

So get excited! The very fact that you have this book in your hands is evidence that you want a more balanced life. You have set your wheels of change in motion, which is the hardest part of the process.

Listening to Yourself

NOW HERE'S THE SECOND THING I'D LIKE YOU TO DO. TRY another visualization exercise, and this one, I promise, you'll like.

Stop wondering what you're going to do to "fix" your problems. And, instead, try to read more slowly, take a breath, and listen.

Really listen, close your eyes, and think only about you for a moment.

Try to shut out the world around you. What I want you to hear is something deep inside you.

Imagine this. Deep inside you, there is a voice crying out. It is a voice that is pleading with you to clean your engine of self-doubt and anxiety. It is a voice begging you to take control of your steering wheel and look for your own road through life.

It is the voice of your true self.

Can you hear it? It is beautiful and soothing. It is also startlingly powerful. And it is ready to change your life forever.

It's hard to believe, isn't it? You may not hear anything yet. That's all right. But for the next several pages, try to pretend that there's another voice inside you other than the one you've been listening to that has been saying you are destined to be the way you are for the rest of your life. Pretend for a moment that there is another voice inside you—the voice of your true self—one that is telling you that you are destined to succeed.

Please, now say it out loud!

I AM destined to succeed. I can choose to succeed!

I'm not kidding. Open your mouth and say the following sentence:

I AM destined to succeed.

Did you say it? Okay, then say it one more time:

I AM destined to succeed.

Does it sound strange coming out of your mouth? Well, we're just getting warmed up. Try this one. And, again, say it out loud:

I AM better than I think.

Say it one more time:

I AM better than I think.

Do you know what you are doing? You are giving yourself "affirmations." Do you remember how in the first chapter I said I didn't believe in affirmations as the be-all and end-all to everything? Then why, you ask, am I asking you to do them now?

Because affirmations are like the spark plugs in your car's

engine. They can give you that special jolt to get you going—to make you realize just what power you have inside you to change your life.

We'll do many more affirmations. I'll warn you again: Affirmations are not going to instantly change our lives. They won't create some miraculous overnight recovery. But they will give us a "shock" of emotional energy. They startle our senses. They will make us begin to break through all that old motor oil and those clogged engine parts that have held us back for so long.

Try this one:

Nothing can stop me.

Now that sounds like something a raving football coach would say at halftime, doesn't it? Again, don't analyze what you're saying. Try not to roll your eyes and wonder what in the world you're doing. Simply place the idea in your mind that once you get your engine started, you're going to go forward at a speed you've never felt before—and nothing is going to stop you!

Nothing can stop me.

Do you realize that most of us spend our entire lives struggling for a little happiness, hoping to see a small glimpse of blue sky against the mass of dark clouds that seems to blanket our lives? What's tragic is that most of us don't realize that we have this power inside us, power that can send us above the clouds to see the blue sky so that we no longer have to push those clouds aside.

We have vast, immeasurable potential that remains untapped within us. Our human minds and spirits can perform miracles if properly used. All we must do is throw off the shackles of our old thinking patterns, and then we will be prepared to rise above the clouds. All we have to do is break from the circumstances around us that have long been determining our attitudes. And then we can bring forth our true inner selves. We can learn to grab hold of that inner self and let it guide our lives. We can learn to be our own person, living above the expectations and demands of others. We can learn to operate at our best—at our actualized potential.

If we don't get to really live our lives, we've lost an incalculable treasure. We've lost the chance to display our astonishing uniqueness—qualities that no one else in this world has. Each of us is a mesh of differing styles, viewpoints, abilities, tastes, and gifts. There's no one in the world who can do what you can do or what I can do, who can think and see the same way you do or I do, who can create what you can create or I can create.

We must recognize that we have far more potential than we even know.

Say it out loud:

I have far more potential than I even know.

Taking Charge of Your Life

YOU MAY BE THINKING, "HEY, JINGER, EASIER SAID THAN done! It's one thing for us to say that we have potential, but how do we start showing it?"

As any salesperson will tell you, the hardest thing about selling is getting started each day. Like any other group of salespeople, our new saleswomen have trouble making that first daily sales call. A saleswoman knows that there's a chance she'll get turned down more than once before the day is over. So it's tough getting started. After all, who wants to head into a day of rejection? I have women tell me they tend to drink an extra cup of coffee each morning, perhaps do some cleaning, or maybe run a couple of errands before doing the first sales call.

I like to share one simple philosophy: **"The only way to start is to start!"** They must simply pick up the phone, call their customers, say "Good morning," and start telling them about the benefits of their products. It's like the sneaker ad: "Just do it!" If they start this way, without a lot of conscious thought, they will soon be breaking the ice, and by the second or third call, they are sharing all the positive attributes of our products, services, and opportunity, and then they actually re-ignite themselves. By reaffirming the power of our opportunity, our Consultants realize they are reaffirming themselves—and by feeling so "up" about who they are, they are much more energized to make the sale.

To improve our lives, we must simply start! We can't wait for the spirit to move us. We can't wait until we feel just right. We need to get going. We can work on our inner life the same way we work a muscle. The more we work on it, the more its performance improves. The more we leave it alone, the more out of shape it gets. Indeed, we can create magic in our own lives simply by believing the phrase "I am responsible." I hate to say it, but that is about as much of a magic formula as I can offer. Until we believe we alone are capable of changing—until we believe in ourselves—then everything else we try is going to be nothing more than a psychological Band-Aid.

Remember this: We are the lead actors in our own particular movie. We either write our own script or we follow the one that has been handed to us. We either choose our fellow actors and actresses, or we let someone else decide who will be onstage with us. Either we direct the action, or someone else who doesn't really know us will do it.

And that's not all. We also have the opportunity to judge our own performance, to write our own reviews—not to let some outside critic do it for us.

We can take complete charge and responsibility of our life and all that happens in it!

That's right. If we want to bring down the curtain right now and rearrange the set, we have the power to do it! If we want to replace the cast or rewrite the script, we have the power to do it! Do you realize the power we have to change the direction of our own lives?

Too many people blame circumstances for their failures. Too many people still think they have no personal power or control. They're wrong. Happiness and success in life do not depend on circumstances but on how we respond to our circumstances. If we set ourselves toward finding the right road, our lives almost automatically begin to change—usually in dramatic ways. We begin waking up with a fire inside and a passion for the day. We feel more productive and confident. We start feeling fulfilled. And we will see that our life has a purpose that is not limited by circumstances. All we have to do is make a commitment to change!

A Commitment to Change

Wait. Let's go back to that last sentence. **A commitment to change?** What does that mean?

It's easy for us to say that we have the desire to change—but developing the strength to change is very, very difficult. The fact is that aiming your car toward the right road takes courage. It requires the death of an old identity and a decision to head into what is essentially the unknown. Sometimes, we have to drive over pretty rough terrain to get onto the right road. We often have to stop and fine-tune our engines a few more times before we get there.

When you add it all up, it really doesn't seem worth the trouble to try something new, right?

Wrong. So many people have wasted so much of their lives by relying on what they perceived was the security of a certain road, only to find that they were on the wrong road and the security was an illusion. They never saw how their lives were slowing down, their inner engines rusting out, their tires going flat. They never found out how capable they could really be. As time went on, they knew something wasn't working, but they wouldn't try to find the problem or the solutions.

And it was all because of the fear of change.

Yes, fear of change is real. Fear is a powerful force that prevents so many of us from getting what we want from life. It stops us from capitalizing on opportunity; it closes our mouths when we want to speak; it wears down our physical vitality; it is what leads to our bouts of worry, tension, embarrassment, panic, and depression. It is the reason why millions of us accomplish little and enjoy less. And we must recognize it exists before we can conquer it.

What we have to do is think of fear as a kind of psychological infection. We cure it the way we cure infections of the body—with specific, proven treatments. When you come across someone who radiates confidence and seems at peace, don't be misled into thinking that the person was just born that way. Don't be disheartened and think, "Gosh, that person must never have known what it's like to feel fear."

The truth is that no one is born with confidence. It's all acquired and developed. The people who are confident developed that skill just as they developed any other. They also developed the ability to beat back fear. As the well-known psychiatrist Dr. Karl Menninger once wrote, "Fears are educated into us. And they can, if we wish, be educated out."

Many of us have fear of failure. We fear that if we try

something and don't succeed, then we will embarrass ourselves. We have let this fear control us for a long, long time.
Do you recall your days back in high school when many of
us felt anxious about preparing for a very difficult exam because of the fear of making a bad grade? I remember studying for an exam with such fear inside me that I could barely
learn the material. I was so focused on the thought that I
might fail that I actually programmed my subconscious to
fail! Do you see how I had put myself into a vicious circle?
Because I was so focused on "not failing," I forgot to focus
on "succeeding." Because I was so focused on avoiding an F,
I couldn't study so I could make an A.

Let me show you another example of how fear causes us
to self-destruct. I've known women who want to be married
so badly that they end up giving off a negative energy that
makes men run away. These are the women who, twenty
minutes into a date, become preoccupied with worry about
whether this relationship will "work." They are so scared of
not being married—they are so caught up in the fear of
being single—that they literally have trouble enjoying being
with a man. They're thinking, "Is this the man I might spend
the rest of my life with? Will we have children? Where will
we live?" Hey, it's just a date—stay in the present!

What if these women simply said, "I'm going to enjoy
myself. I'm going to treat the man with me tonight as a
great human being, and I will have complete confidence that
everything will work out for the best, even if we never see
each other again." After all, didn't our mothers tell us that
love happens when we're not trying to make it happen?

Do You Fear Success?

WHAT FEW OF US REALIZE IS THAT THERE IS NOTHING more crippling than fear. Fear produces something like a "brain lock," in which our minds just don't think right. When we act out of fear, we tend not to see how a problem can be turned around. We don't seem to be aware of the other roads there are in life.

And, like a virus, fear can seep into every facet of our lives. Significantly, many of us fear *success!* Success sometimes is more frightening than failure!

When I stand before new saleswomen and discuss the fear of success, I get a lot of blank looks. Invariably, someone will say, "But, Jinger, the reason I'm here is because I want to be a success. I don't understand why you are associating the word 'fear' with the word 'success.' " What I try to explain is that some of us don't grow up with an image of ourselves as very smart or capable. So, as we start to grow beyond our internal negative self-images, we are actually unsettling the foundation upon which we have built our self-image. Subconsciously, we become uncomfortable, because we do not know what to do without those familiar negative voices that tell us we are not all that competent. When we bring success into our lives and start transforming ourselves, we ironically feel greater levels of anxiety. The reason is because success is a very new and unfamiliar experience for many of us.

Do you realize what that means? Because we want to avoid anxiety—because we want to stay in our safety zones—we stop growing and changing! In other words: **We begin to fear the possibility of success!**

I know one very capable woman on the fast track of a major corporation who told me that she sometimes wondered if she really wanted to become president of that corporation.

"Why?" I asked.

"Well, I'll have to start speaking before large groups," she said. "I'll have to manage others, produce annual reports, be responsible to stockholders. And I think, 'Hey, that's overwhelming! That's way too much for me to handle!' "

I smiled and told her about how Dick and I had decided in 1986 to take our company public. Here I was, suddenly chairman of a public company, and I didn't even have a financial background. "But you know what?" I said to this woman. "It's the growing and the learning that was exciting. I learned what I had to learn."

"But I don't know—," the woman said.

"Look, you've been able to handle everything that's been thrown at you so far!" I said. "Why do you think you couldn't handle something different?"

She paused. "Jinger, I just don't know," she said.

I think I know: fear of the unknown. After listening to one of my talks, one very well-dressed woman named Aileen came up to me and told me about a recurring nightmare she had. In her dream, she said, she would be in a car, driving smoothly along a highway, until she got to a particular point where lanes opened out to many on and off ramps. Everything looked confusing and frightening to her, and the thought of so many options terrified her. She felt the only way to deal with this terror was by pulling her car over to the side of the road—and coming to a complete stop!

"At the end of the dream, I'm stuck in my car, watching other cars race past me," the woman said. "Jinger, it's a nightmare! It's like I'm frozen!"

I understood exactly what she was talking about. There's

something comforting about the illusion that life simply consists of one simple narrow road. There's something comforting about the idea that we can remain in a little cocoon. Of course, almost none of us admits that out loud. We cloak our fears in perfectly reasonable-sounding excuses. We talk about circumstances beyond our control. We say we don't have time to be successful, that we don't have the skills to be successful, that we don't have the support from our family.

What we're afraid to admit is that we're *afraid*. We just drift along, being carried wherever the road takes us. It's crazy! Although doing nothing results in the greatest failure of all, it apparently is easier for many of us to accept passive rather than active failure.

Questions to Break Your Fear

D O YOU WONDER IF FEAR CONTROLS YOUR LIFE, ESPE-cially when it comes to growth or change? Perhaps these scenarios and questions will help you decide.

1. *Think of being the first person on the dance floor at a wedding reception. You love the music, but you don't want to risk enjoying it because you worry that people will stare at you and think you look foolish when you dance. What would you do? Would you rather not do something than risk the disapproval of others?*

2. *Let's say your husband or a friend asks you what you want to do tonight. You reply, "Oh, it doesn't matter, whatever you want to do." So the other person says, "Fine, I want to go to an adventure movie." You are now stuck going to a movie you don't want to see, and you feel resentful about it. Ask yourself: If you really want something, do you have trouble asking for it?*

3. Step inside your closet. Do you have dresses that you've never worn—and thus never enjoyed—because you say to yourself that you must "save" them for a special occasion? What if you died tomorrow? Who would wear that great dress?

4. Do you talk yourself out of buying a fine antique table because you think something might happen to it in your home?

5. Do you ever talk yourself out of a relationship because you think the person is out of your league (too attractive, too successful, too rich)?

6. Do you talk yourself out of trying a new activity simply because you don't want to look incompetent in front of other people (e.g., skiing, tennis, windsurfing, golf, horseback riding)?

7. Do you tell yourself that you can't lose weight because you don't have the willpower? Or because your metabolism doesn't work the way it did when you were younger?

8. Do you ever say to yourself that you're too old to try something new?

9. Do you believe you don't have enough time to master something new, even though medical studies now say a fifty-year-old female without cancer or heart disease will probably live to the age of ninety-two?

10. Do you have difficulty enjoying a pleasurable moment because you constantly think about what you should be doing instead?

The Courage to Dare

*I*F YOU FIND YOURSELF ANSWERING YES TO ANY OF THESE QUES-
tions, you're in the same position as just about every
woman you meet. We each must learn how to tap into
our hidden sources of strength so that we can overcome our
fears and aim ourselves toward the most rewarding roads in
life. Instead of taking the familiar and ultimately unfulfilling
roads, we can develop the confidence to drive on those unfamiliar yet ultimately thrilling roads—the ones that let us
be successful and express our feelings.

Initially, it will seem impossible to believe that if you keep
on the uncomfortable road, you will become happier,
healthier, and more successful. The truth is that you will at
first feel anxious and ill at ease on this new journey. Your
stomach might feel squeamish and your head a little dizzy.
You may look in the rearview mirror and wonder whether
you should put your car in reverse and get back on the safe,
comfortable, boring road.

You may be scared.

**But if you just keep going a little bit farther, one day at a time,
a whole new horizon will begin to open.**

"Do the thing you fear and the death of fear is certain,"
Ralph Waldo Emerson wrote. The Danish philosopher Søren
Kierkegaard declared, "To venture is to risk anxiety, but not
to venture is to lose yourself." These great men aren't just
making abstract philosophical statements. They understand
that when we face our fears, the range of possibilities for
discovering who we can be is endless. By breaking from the
cage of fear, we discover our full potential. We discover that
there are no ceilings on our talent. By facing our fears, we
can energize ourselves for the pursuit of our own goals. **We
don't have to spend our life stuck in old patterns because we now**

have the courage to dare to do anything. The more we face and overcome what we're afraid of, the easier it becomes to accomplish great things. Interestingly enough, working through your fear of just one thing in your life subconsciously makes you less afraid of the other things that you thought you were afraid of, too.

Here's a practical example of what I'm talking about. I have a friend named Jane who is utterly brilliant in many areas. Literally, she can do whatever she wants. There's only one problem. She's scared to death about standing up and giving a speech in public.

One day, I said to her, "Jane, there's only one way of dealing with that fear. You're going to have to immerse yourself in your fear."

I admit, it sounds difficult. After all, logic says if you're scared of doing something, then you shouldn't do it. But here's where that logic is wrong. The only way to change yourself is to put yourself in a position in which you face your fear. In Jane's case, she had to give a speech in public in order to beat back her fear of public speaking.

I know some of you have this very fear. And, let me tell you, your first speech, when you do it, will not be perfect. You may sweat and stammer and feel completely embarrassed. So what should you do next?

Give another speech. That's right. After you have risked carrying out one speech, the next one will be somewhat more familiar. Your third speech will be even less frightening. And by your fourth or fifth, you will discover, to your delight, that an audience finds you a skilled speaker. Like an athlete in training, you will have improved your skills. And it would never have happened unless you had first decided to put yourself into the position that you feared most.

Often, our new saleswomen tell us they're terrified of approaching a stranger to introduce her to our products. We nod understandingly and then tell them that we don't want them to approach just one stranger. We want them to approach five strangers!

The fact is, some of our saleswomen never try to approach strangers. But the ones who do find themselves going through a startling transformation. The first couple of times the saleswomen introduce themselves, they are usually stiff and uncomfortable. By the fifth time, they are becoming very confident. They are starting to realize how much more rewarding it is to develop some successful new behaviors than to keep traveling on the same old road. What's more, they soon realize they can beat back their inner sense of failure. That's one of the most powerful feelings in all of humankind.

The Road to Wholeness

*I*F YOU'RE NOT WILLING TO EMBRACE YOUR FEARS, THEN YOU may want to close this book right now. Thanks for buying it, but it isn't going to help you. The reason: There is no magic formula for change except the willingness to change. **And that means the *willingness* to take a risk and do something about your fears.**

It's like learning to snow ski. If you've ever tried to do it, then you know that to ski, you have to lean forward and feel as if you're falling downhill. If you want to be a good skier, you have to lean past what is called the "fall line." The problem is that most of us have spent our lives trying not to fall. It's our instinct to fight against gravity. As a result, when we're on a hill learning to snow ski, we naturally lean back into the hill—which makes us terrible skiers. Only when we "act out" our fear—when we go with gravity and ski in a way that makes us think we're going to fall—do we realize we will not fall at all! We actually flow down the hill without resistance.

One of the reasons Outward Bound programs are so popular with business executives is that people come back realizing that even small attempts to confront their fears and take risks do wonders for their self-esteem. In these programs, they are alone in the wilderness, or they try to climb a huge mountain, or they raft down a wild river. Even if they are not 100 percent successful in achieving their goal, they feel wondrously alive from the risks they have taken. Their adrenaline races and their hearts beat faster. They know that by immersing themselves in their fears, they have touched a great, vibrant power deep inside them. And when they go back to their real lives, they now know that fear is not bad—that it can be the source of energy and exhilaration. By taking a risk in one area, they become more confident about taking a risk in another.

Indeed, regardless of where we are in life, we can make significant changes by initially taking very small risks, and then moving to larger ones. For instance, if you fear intimate communication with people—if you are sometimes the Caged Spirit described in the last chapter who has trouble verbalizing what you want out of life—then your first risk might be calling a woman you know well, asking her to lunch, and telling a story about yourself that you previously felt too shy to reveal. Later, when you realize the lunch went just fine, you will feel more confident about taking a larger risk and talking more openly to people you don't know well.

Throughout history, great thinkers have tried to define courage. I like to think of courage as nothing more than recognizing that we are fearful about something and doing it anyway. If there is a single piece of advice I would like you to remember, it is to never be afraid of fear. As you start changing, don't run from your fear, but move toward it and even embrace it. Remember, the more we try to avoid or resist the things that scare us, the more we stay the same.

Please, don't turn around even if the road right now seems uncomfortable and a little scary. We're headed toward wholeness, and it's going to be the greatest ride you could ever imagine.

High-Octane Gasoline

Giving Your Life a Jolt of Self-Esteem

We can decide to wallow in self-pity and sorrow, or we can

decide that we have self-worth that cannot be affected by anyone

or by any outside circumstances.

BESIDES EMBRACING OUR FEARS, THERE'S ANOTHER THING WE must do if we want to make healthy progress on our road through life.

We must learn again to love ourselves.

This may sound so elementary that it's almost not worth discussing. But the fact is that few of us really love ourselves anymore. It's not enough just to like ourselves. **We must love ourselves.**

I'm not talking about narcissistic self-love. I'm talking about a genuine love of who we are—a genuine love of our own uniqueness.

God did not make us to be like anyone else. Geneticists say that the odds of our parents having another child like us are 1 in 102 billion. **The combination of attributes that constitutes us will never be duplicated!** The environment and temperament of each living thing is unique! If you treat yourself as the most important person in your life, you can nurture yourself to wholeness, and create a truly peaceful and happy life.

Now let's stop for a moment. How many of us really believe that last sentence? Because so many of us expect failure, disappointment, and put-downs in life, we forget that we have been created in a special and beautiful way. Because we have spent so long fixating on what we think we can't do, we forget what we really can do! The idea of loving ourselves deeply may sound funny.

Some of us don't even know what it's like to think well about ourselves. Take this little test to see if I'm right:

First say, **I like myself.**

Now say, **I love myself.**

Ask yourself which sentence was more comfortable for you to say. For most of us, it was the first one.

Now let's make it harder. Imagine saying those same two sentences to someone else. Telling another person that you like yourself is one thing, but isn't it much harder to deal with the idea of telling someone that you love yourself? Does it sound too self-serving?

How to Learn to Love Yourself

*I*T'S BEEN THAT WAY FOR A LOT OF US FOR A LONG, LONG time. Do you remember how as children we may have learned that we would receive more attention for getting hurt, being sick, not cleaning our plate, leaving our room messy, or getting into trouble rather than by behaving well? With repeated mental imprinting, we set up a system whereby we received more attention for our *negative self* rather than our *positive self.*

Nor were many of us taught what internalized self-esteem was all about. If you go to a party, for example, and ask people about their lives, you can almost be certain that they will tell you what they "do" for a living instead of who they "are."

Obviously, there's nothing wrong with being proud of your profession—as long as you know your identity is not tied solely to what you do. But, for a lot of us, our sense of self—and self-esteem—is very limited. We often evaluate ourselves through something external—through a prop. When I grew up, I believed people in fancy cars must be better people. In the same way, many people today use fancy material things to feel better about themselves. Our feelings of self-esteem often hinge on what we possess or who we associate with or where we work. We permit our feelings about ourselves to rise or fall depending on what others think about us. And we women have it especially tough because we often live with the assumption that we must be focused consistently on the needs of those around us. We are well trained to put others first: we feel we must be selfless in our roles as mothers, daughters, sisters, wives, lovers, or friends. We confuse our true value as human beings with our achievements or the way we are perceived by others. We try to conform to

94

other people's values or society's values rather than feeling inwardly valuable simply because we exist!

In other words, we depend on *externalized* self-esteem. We don't know how to look inside ourselves for happiness and fulfillment.

We forget how to love ourselves.

Imagine that our self-esteem is like an exquisite, sparkling painted coating on the outside of our cars. If it's chipped over and over again, it's no longer smooth, and rust can begin to erode the finish. Soon, everything is falling apart. Without self-esteem, we become even more afraid to leave our safe "roles." Without self-esteem, we don't ever realize that we can change completely.

And, indeed, we will not change until we believe—truly believe—that we are *worthy* of whatever pursuits we choose in life. We must believe we have a *core value* that must be protected like a precious gem.

If we realize that we have something very valuable to honor deep inside ourselves, then our lives will change forever from this moment forward. It is like being dressed in a very fine garment. We are more careful to keep it clean than if we are dressed casually. When we buy a new car, we wash and wax it and avoid any potential scrapes. As the car gets older, we tend to neglect it. We think it's not as valuable or that it's no longer a thing worth preserving perfectly.

We act the same way with our own lives. We think, "Well, we've come this far and haven't accomplished all that much." We think we're like a used car: we don't have the value we once did. We think we're too old or too out of shape or too uneducated or too *whatever* to make a difference. Without that sense of self-esteem—without that fervent belief in our own value—we are prone to do destructive things or allow ourselves to waste away emotionally.

Do you remember that exercise I asked you to do in the previous chapter in which you were to stop and listen for your inner voice? Here's some great news. That voice hasn't gone away! We just have to turn up its volume. It is right inside us, telling us that there is nothing that can hold us back, that we are destined to succeed, to celebrate the wonders of our life and our world. It is telling us that we deserve to have everything we want in life. It is telling us that we can cherish every moment as a special one. And it is telling us that attaining our goals is simply a matter of believing in ourselves and then taking action to accomplish them.

We do not have to get the right job, improve our social status, or lose weight in order to get self-esteem. Our self-esteem has been inside us all along. No matter how old we are, no matter what has happened to us in the past, no matter how many dents we have in our exteriors—we are still God's unique creation!

Remember, all dents are repairable!

The Return of Your Self-Esteem

I SUSPECT THAT YOU MAY HAVE PICKED UP THIS BOOK BECAUSE you, like me, want the best life has to offer. You want to learn and grow. Or it could be that you felt depressed or unsatisfied with a relationship. Perhaps your children were driving you crazy, your family or friendships were disappointing, or you wished you could find a more satisfying career. You might have bought this book because you wished you had the inner strength to achieve your goals. Or maybe you have been wondering why you have a constant nagging belief that your life is not as valuable as it could be.

Whatever our specific issue is, the truth is that none of us can resolve anything until we bring our own self-esteem back to life. Until we learn to love ourselves again.

Say this sentence out loud:

I am the most important person in my life!

You are! You are the center of your own existence! To possess this sense of self doesn't mean you are being selfish. You are not being morally reprehensible. You are simply connecting with the most spiritual side of yourself and realizing that you matter! You matter not because you are beautiful or smart or rich—but because you exist. You are precious simply because of the fact that you are alive! Now say it out loud:

I matter! I am precious!

Great athletes have always understood this concept. They know that what separates the winners from the "also-rans" is the tremendous power of the mind. Those who win *believe* they can win. They believe they *deserve* to win. Indeed, they train their minds to win as much as they train their bodies. Nothing holds them back—not the fear of the contest, not the importance of the competition, not the exhausting nature of the contest to come. And, most significantly, they don't start feeling like winners only after they have won a championship. **They understood they were champions before the game even got started!**

And that's what we must do, too. To be successful at anything, we have to tap into our self-esteem and realize we already are successful. It makes no difference if others find us to be a success if we do not think of ourselves as a success. It makes no difference whether others respect us if we don't respect ourselves. It makes no difference how much others love us if we do not love ourselves. What matters is that our lives be "inner-directed" (driven by our own sense of self-esteem), rather than "other-directed" (driven by the attitudes of others).

How Much Self-Esteem Do You Have?

D O YOU HAVE THE NECESSARY SELF-ESTEEM TO MOVE FOR-ward in life? Perhaps your answers to these questions will help you decide.

1. Do you notice the flaws in your surroundings? Or do you find delight in the beauty of natural wonders around you?

2. Are you so bogged down with judgments and questions that you have difficulty letting yourself experience pleasure? Or do you channel your thoughts and words into uplifting and encouraging ideas and observations?

3. Do you feel "weighted down" with burdens from the past, such as unresolved conflicts or old tragedies? Or do you concentrate on experiencing the rewards of the present?

4. Do you shrug off compliments? Or do you accept them graciously with an immediate "Thank you"?

5. When playing a sport like tennis, do you say "I'm sorry" after every flubbed ball? Or do you laugh at your mistakes and relish the joy of the exercise, the companionship, or the weather?

6. At a large social gathering, do you try to remain inconspicuous? Or do you enjoy the idea of conversing with new people?

7. Do you spend an inordinate amount of time buying a present for someone else and then worry that it will not be good enough? Or do you pick out a present that you think is just right and then give it to that person with great enthusiasm?

8. Do you create an artificial cutoff for your life by saying things like "After the age of forty, I won't look so good?" Or do you appreciate whatever age you are and then focus on ways to become wiser, more special, and even more at peace?

9. When you finally get what you think you wanted, do you discover that you're still not happy? Or have you spent the time to determine what you really want out of life?

10. Are you scared that life is someday going to pass you by? Or do you possess an upbeat, optimistic attitude about the future?

Focusing on Your Positives

I DON'T THINK IT'S AN EXAGGERATION TO SAY THAT WE COULD all use more self-esteem. The old adage "Know yourself" doesn't just mean "Know only your negative self." It means knowing your positive qualities, especially when you go through painful times.

There are plenty of people who believe they are unhappy simply because they have been focusing on the negative aspects of their lives. They fixate on things that are wrong in their jobs or their relationships. They know all about the "circumstances" that have made them unhappy. But their hearts quickly change once they start looking at the good things surrounding them—when they realize that almost every experience has positive elements. In fact, every moment of our lives is worth celebrating. Through the habit of positive focusing, we reap tremendous rewards.

There was one psychologist I have read about who relied on a single technique to deal with people who were depressed. He didn't try to discuss in depth with his patients the reasons for their depression. He simply would ask them to describe one small thing they were good at doing—and then he would encourage them to do that. If they couldn't tell him of one good thing, he would visit their homes and take a tour, looking for a clue that he could use to help them out of their depression.

On one occasion, the psychologist visited an isolated woman whose only human contact was with people on Sunday mornings at church and her gardener. Although the psychologist noticed the house was dingy, he saw in the kitchen window some beautiful African violets. Knowing that African violets were difficult to grow, he gave the woman a task. He told her to take several cuttings of African violets, nurture them into adult plants, and then send one of her violets to a church member whenever there was an announcement of a christening, an engagement, an illness, or a death. Then the psychologist headed toward the door.

"But what about a therapy session?" the woman cried.

"We've just had it," he said.

A few years later, according to the article I read, the woman died. A headline in the local paper read "African Violet Queen Will Be Missed by Thousands."

Without even talking about her despair, that psychologist had picked out the one bright spot in this lonely woman's life and helped her touch it. She recognized her own self-worth and realized she was valuable! That one act did more for her emotional state of being than a year of therapy could hope to do.

Exercises to Build Your Self-Esteem

IF WE HAVE BEEN SO SUCCESSFUL AT CREATING OUR OWN NEGative self-image, then doesn't it stand to reason that we can create positive self-esteem, too? We absolutely can—

and here's how to get started. Try one or more of these exercises that are destined to build self-esteem.

1. *Write out a list of your positive accomplishments from the past. Don't be discriminating: the small accomplishments are just as important as the big ones. Next, write down all the positive characteristics in your personality. Finally, add a third list of some of your most pleasant experiences in life. Stick the lists on a bulletin board or on a refrigerator door—someplace you will see it and be able to read it every day! Whenever anything negative creeps into your mind, read your lists. Just reading these lists will raise your spirits and elevate your self-esteem at times when they badly need lifting.*

2. *Write a sixty-second commercial about yourself. The point of this exercise is to get you to try to sell yourself to an audience you don't know, and you have about 150 words to tell that audience about the positive side of yourself. In this commercial, you're not allowed to tell the audience what you want to be. You must tell them only who you are right now. You can write about your integrity, your sense of humor, your ability to get along with other people, your creative side— whatever! Once you're finished, stand up and read the commercial out loud. And make sure you communicate this commercial in a way to make your unknown audience realize that you genuinely love who you are!*

3. *Be around positive people. It's true, positive attitudes are contagious. The more you're around people who are brimming with self- esteem, the more you find the self-esteem in yourself. If you associate with negative people, you will inevitably focus on the gloomy side of life. You will allow all kinds of psychologically harmful junk informa- tion to penetrate your mind. Avoid the type of people who gossip, repeat rumors, snipe about others, and in general act miserable with their* place in the world. Be around people who celebrate you! Be around people who look for the good in others and in life! Be around people who smile at you in a way that makes you feel valued!

4. *Accept a compliment.* That isn't as easy as it sounds. The next time someone compliments you, listen to the compliment and believe it as being absolutely true. If someone says he or she appreciates your considerate manners, then stop for a second and say, "Thank you." It's almost an instant confirmation. You believe the other person and it helps you believe it about yourself.

5. Finally, repeat affirmations to yourself, even if you're not sure you believe them. Remember, affirmations are like spark plugs that ignite your engine. And repeating affirmations out loud penetrates and convinces your mind that you do have great value. I know people who affirm themselves out loud every morning while driving. With affirmations, it's important to go back to the core of your existence— to recognize that even your smallest acts have God's value in them. Some people begin a day of affirmations by praising the simplest elements of their being. They say such things as "I can laugh," "I can feel," "I can hear and touch and walk."

These kinds of exercises are remarkably empowering, especially for those of you having trouble thinking of positive things to say about yourself.

Affirmation Exercises

BELOW, I'VE GIVEN YOU A LIST OF POTENTIAL AFFIRMA-tions. They always are framed in the present tense, to emphasize that this is the way we are now, not the way we might be *someday*. If these aren't accurate for your particular circumstances, then substitute positive descriptions that realistically fit your life. Remember, the goal of affirmations is not to make you feel uncomfortable, but to feel energized. They don't have to be long or drawn out. They can be brief, strong messages that lock into your subconscious.

As you read these, speak aloud slowly and sincerely. Remember to speak s-l-o-w-l-y!

I am deserving!

I am totally unique!

I am lovable and loved!

I am well intentioned!

I am willing!

I am me!

I am the best me!

I was created for good!

I am growing!

I am learning!

I am discovering all the good that life has to offer!

I am attractive!

I am healthy!

I am fun to be with!

I am worthy of happiness!

God sees only GOOD in me!

You don't have to make your affirmations so general. Nor do you have to make them particularly profound. Often, I like to say very specific things to myself that make me feel good about who I am. Even the most minor affirmations can shatter our negative thinking patterns. Here are some examples of good things.

I have good friends.

I have good luck.

I am trustworthy.

I am honest.

I smile at strangers.

I am good company.

I am generous.

Finally, try making affirmations that are in many ways similar to prayer. In the mornings, I make statements about my belief in the day that is about to unfold. Here is an example of what I'll say:

"There's a reason I woke today. There's a plan for me, and whatever unfolds for me today, I know I can handle it. God has created me. Any problems that come my way are my opportunity to grow. Change is inevitable and, knowing that, I can accept change."

And in the evenings, no matter how bad the day has turned out, I take the time to deposit good thoughts in my brain so that I sleep and dream about positive things. Basically, I want to remind myself of what I have to be thankful for that day:

I am thankful for the health and safety of my family today.

I am thankful for the health and safety of my friends today.

I am thankful I was able to respond to a difficult situation today.

I am thankful I was able to solve some problems today.

I am thankful to be alive.

Finally, we can do other affirmations with body language alone. Right now, as you're reading this, stop for just a moment and smile. Even if you don't feel like smiling, just go ahead and do it. Take a deep, relaxing breath and smile.

Are you noticing how that smile changes your state of mind? You're not waiting for someone or something to make you happy. You're making the choice to smile. You're making the choice to be happy.

Getting Better Gas Mileage

RIGHT NOW, OUR CONSCIOUS MINDS MAY BE THINKING, "IT seems so ridiculous to repeat affirmations out loud!" But if we will simply trust the process of believing in ourselves, our own subconscious minds will soon get the message and begin working for us. According to numerous Eastern religions and philosophies, once we state something ten thousand times, it becomes a mantra, forming and molding who we are. I'm not advocating any particular religion, but I do know that when we regularly affirm ourselves, we start touching a powerful place inside us. Even when you seem overwhelmed with problems, you'll find great power in being able to see a glass as half full instead of half empty.

If you'll allow me to use another automobile analogy, our thoughts are like the quality of gasoline we put in our engines. Obviously, if we fill up our engines with impure, dirty gasoline, they are soon going to be a mess, barely wheezing along. Likewise, if we are constantly depositing negative thoughts in our minds, then we are producing needless wear and tear on our mental motors. We will be overwhelmed by anxiety, frustration, and feelings of inferiority. We will take any unpleasant or discouraging situation to heart, pulling off to the side of the road so we can dwell on the unpleasant.

The fact is that our subconscious believes whatever happens to be poured into it. So if it is being pumped full of negative thoughts, then it naturally is going to begin to think negatively. It starts backfiring with the message that we are unsure and helpless, incompetent or incapable. But if we put in high-octane gasoline, our engines start working. If we take charge of our subconscious—if we let only the best thoughts enter—we will be on our way to happiness and serenity.

We can decide to wallow in self-pity and sorrow, or we can decide that we have self-worth that cannot be affected by anyone or by any outside circumstances. A healthy self-esteem not only brings great freedom from self-sabotage, but it also helps ward off additional problems before they have the chance to materialize. Indeed, dwelling on our limitations will lead us straight down the road to mediocrity and failure. What's more, our body is affected in negative ways when we practice negative thinking. But constantly reminding ourselves that we really are valuable will make us even more successful than in our wildest dreams. **If we think we deserve respect—and if we treat ourselves with respect—then others will treat us with respect, too.** Our self-esteem—our ability to love ourselves—can be one of the strongest forces in the universe!

A Clean Windshield
6

Setting Your Sights on the Journey Ahead

We can turn our minds into great motivational centers that will

provide encouragement and inspiration and keep us aimed in the

right direction. With positive thinking, we can believe that today

is going to be a great day and that tomorrow will be

even greater.

THIS CHAPTER IS GOING TO PUT US TO WORK. IN THE NEXT FEW
pages, we're going to take a lifetime of small habits and put
them aside!

Chapter 5 got us off to a good start, but changing our lives
will take more than developing a new outlook. **Positive thinking is not the end-all to our problems.** *Positive action is!*

If positive thinking alone could be translated into joy and

contentment, then why hasn't the quotient of unhappiness in this world been significantly lowered? After all, the power of positive thinking is not a new idea. The concept has been with us as far back as the Bible **("If thou canst believe, all things are possible to him that believeth"),** and there have been so many "positive thinking" movements in this country that it's hard to keep count of them. Did you know that there was a time in the 1920s when people all over America were murmuring to themselves the phrase invented by Émile Coué, a French psychotherapist, that went, "Every day, and in every way, I am becoming better and better." Today, more than eight million copies have been printed of Norman Vincent Peale's *The Power of Positive Thinking*, which was first published in 1952.

Yet despite all the literature, it remains a real challenge for us to learn how to love ourselves deeply. Why? Because very well-intentioned people still sabotage their own *positive thoughts* with *negative actions*. We must stay committed to the process of change. We must make the effort to learn new positive habits that can transform the way we act.

The success of our new journey depends on our ability to link positive thinking with positive action! It's only through steady reconditioning of the mind that we can learn to act positively and without limitations. It's not enough for us to head off down our new road with a vague notion about the "will" to change. Yes, our newfound positive thinking will certainly get us moving forward, but we'll never get up to speed unless we have a constructive plan of action—a road map, if you will. Now that we believe we-can-do-it, it's time for the how-to-do-it to emerge.

Remember, we are attempting to eliminate a lifetime of negative habits and belief systems. Nurturing ourselves in this new way involves letting go of some lifelong assumptions about the "shoulds" and "ought tos" in our lives. As you'll later see, it will even mean letting go of the way we phrase basic sentences about who we are and what we are destined to become! It means we must be willing to be beginners again, no matter what our age is or what our life has been about up until this very moment.

On this new journey, we have the most powerful force on our side—our minds! I promise you, there is nothing more powerful than our minds—once they are focused. Our minds can create the response we want to any situation. As the ancient proverb goes, "If you conquer your mind, you conquer the world."

Listening for Our Positive Voice

SADLY, MANY OF US HAVE LET OUR MINDS WANDER. WE have allowed them to remain uncultivated and unchallenged. We have allowed negativity to creep in. We have not focused our minds on the issues that can transform our inner being.

As I said in the last chapter, if you want a successful life, then you cannot afford negative thoughts. Every thought must be one that will take us farther along the road to a better life. We must demand only the highest-octane gasoline for our inner engines. If we can train our minds to act this way, then we can turn any circumstance, no matter how unfortunate or disappointing, into a positive, success-oriented experience. We can't control what happens to us, but we can control our response to it. By responding to life with positive energy—by turning positive thinking into positive action—we can find greater peace of mind, and lifelong success. **All we have to do is get control of our minds!**

Let's say it another way. We all have thousands of thoughts a day—and, yes, some of them are negative. But the negative thoughts we have can hurt us only if we put them into action. There is no reason why a negative thought has to stay in us. If we want, we can send it straight to our exhaust system and get it out of our cars entirely!

Furthermore, we can learn to direct our inner thoughts and spoken words toward *positive behavior*. We can turn our minds into great motivational centers that will provide encouragement and inspiration and keep us aimed in the right direction. With positive thinking, we can believe that today is going to be a great day and that tomorrow will be even greater. And, then, with positive action, we will make sure that it happens. We will make sure our dreams come true.

The Substitution Principle

HOW CAN WE TAKE THE NEGATIVES IN OUR LIVES AND turn them into positives? It's a lot easier now that we have already begun to learn to connect with our true inner voice. You see, every time we hear a negative voice in our heads, all we need to do is keep adjusting the volume until we are tuned in only to the voice of our true selves. When we hear the negative voice of criticism, we must stop and recognize that we have another voice to hear: our true voice of encouragement. When we hear the old negative voice of complaint, we simply must listen for the voice of comfort. When our negative voice is trying to persuade us that we are not blessed and unhappy, we can rest assured that our true voice is telling us something entirely different—that we are special and unique. All we have to do is hear it, or refocus our thinking until we can hear it.

I am well aware that many of us have become so accustomed to listening to our negative voices that we don't think we can achieve anything worthwhile. We may think that no matter how successful we become, we will always be burdened by those little voices telling us that we're not good enough, or our lives are not what they should be, or that we can't achieve any great accomplishments. Some of us think it's perfectly natural to feel down on ourselves.

But those negative voices can be interrupted! We can learn to turn the volume down initially and then eventually turn off those voices forever. **We have the power to destroy negative voices!**

Here's how we're going to do it. The essence of our strategy is to substitute a positive, empowering thought for a negative one. It has been said by one writer that our minds are like giant slide projectors. Just as a projector can hold one slide at a time, so do our minds hold only one thought at a time. If that's the case, then our goal is to hit the click button when a negative thought comes on-screen and quickly replace it with a positive one.

The more we work at empowering ourselves with positive thoughts, the more we will be able to avoid putting any unpleasant, negative thoughts on the screen at all. We'll soon be able to spot our negative voice the moment it starts, and we'll be able to cut off that voice instead of letting it run its entire destructive course. We'll be focusing our mind by showing it only strong, positive images. In time, our minds will be conditioned for the positive! Positively You! You cannot imagine how ecstatic you will feel when you do this!

How do we start replacing the negative with the positive? One of the most effective ways to start is by listening to ourselves talk. That's right. It is impossible for negative thoughts to stay only in our brains. They inevitably come out in our speech. Negative thoughts will even come out sandwiched between positive words.

So at the very outset, it's important we do our best to avoid any negative speech. For instance, I try not to describe myself with any words that end with "n't." I avoid sentences that begin with the words "I can't," "I won't," "I shouldn't," and "I couldn't." I try to stay away from words like "never" and "always." Have you ever heard the saying "Never say 'never,' because it always comes back to get you"? It's true. Absolute or extreme words can lock us into a destructive frame of mind.

In essence, it's critical that we attempt to *revoice* the way we feel about ourselves, regardless of the circumstances. If you follow these techniques, you will begin to turn off those negative voices, and you will experience positive growth that you haven't known before.

LABELITIS

I USED TO REPRIMAND MYSELF IMMEDIATELY IF I MADE A MIS-take. And I'd do it by using a negative label. If I messed up at work, for example, I would respond by saying, "How could I be so dumb?" If I missed a deadline on a major project, I used to say, "I'm not capable!" Or if I got lost while driving, I'd snap, "I'm so stupid!"

Were these harmless little comments just to relieve the pressure? No, these reprimands were far more devastating than I knew. What I was doing was programming my mind to think my mistakes were a definitive sign that I was an incapable person.

Please, mistakes are just that—mistakes! When things happen, we simply need to state, "I made a mistake. Now how can I fix it?" We take responsibility for that one mistake, try to fix it to the best of our ability, and, in the process, learn how not to do it again. The key is using mistakes as an opportunity to grow, not as an opportunity to engage in what I call "Labelitis."

Today, whenever I experience a temporary failure or setback in my life, I refuse to get upset and call myself dumb, stupid, incompetent, or any other label. I ask myself what evidence there is to possibly support the idea that I am dumb. And, of course, under that scrutiny, there is no evidence at all. I literally say things to myself as obvious as this: "Hey, I'm not dumb. I just wasn't paying attention and I made a mistake." Every time I do that, I am taking one more blow at the negative voice that has been inside me for years. I am telling myself that I am human and that I will get some dents in my car—yet I am also saying that deep down, I'm a capable, positive person.

Try this exercise to turn your reprimands around:

1. *On a sheet of paper, list the negative things you tend to say to yourself whenever you make a mistake or "think" you look foolish. (Examples are: "I never get it right!" "I'm always like this!")*

2. *Then, next to that negative statement, write a positive statement. Give yourself a positive trait that is as nearly opposite to the negative trait you have just written down. If you tend to say "I am a fool" when you experience a failure, then write down as your opposite statement, "I am a smart and competent person because I have the ability to learn." If you say "I wish I could be like Susan," then write down as your opposite statement, "I am glad I am different from Susan because we are both unique and have special, different talents."*

Do you see how to do the exercise? You might think you're fooling yourself with your "positive" statements, but by writing them down, you will realize just how much you want to be that type of person. And you will also realize that the negative "label" hardly captures who you really are.

SAY "I CAN"

ONE OF THE BIG CHALLENGES IN LIFE IS LEARNING HOW TO CON-quer the phrase "I can't" and replacing it with the phrase "I can." Incredibly, almost all of our beliefs that we are unable to do something started with the sentence that began "I can't . . ."

Just the phrase alone, even when used in the most innocu-ous circumstances, leads us to think that we are incapable of performing the behavior in question. For example, some of us tend to say, "I'm sorry, I *can't* have lunch tomorrow" or "I *can't* make that meeting tonight," even when that's just not true. We are not incapable of having lunch or going to a meeting. We *choose* not to. But instead of saying "choose," we say "I can't." And that helps perpetuate the negative voice in our brain that says we are *incapable!*

You might think this is a small point, but what we must remember is that our subconscious handles messages in ways we don't expect. Throughout the day, if our subcon-scious is constantly hearing us say, "I can't," then it becomes imprinted with the message of incapability. If we say, "I can't stop smoking," we not only are telling ourselves a lie—any-one who starts smoking can certainly stop!—but we also are sending our subconscious one more message that we are unable to change something about ourselves.

Soon, we give up trying to change. And, at that point, our "I can't" voice begins to dominate us, making us think that all of our desires are beyond our grasp. The "I can't" voice will start to dictate who we are and who we aren't, what we can do and what we are capable of having in life. And it's all because we got into the habit of saying, "I can't."

Usually, when I enter a period in life that I know is going to be difficult—when a deadline hits for a major work project or when I'm attempting to learn a new skill—I begin by saying, "I can learn!" "I can achieve what I want!" "I can make a difference!" I know the "I can't" voice is lurking in my mind, looking for the opportunity to dissuade me from even attempting success. So when I hear that voice, I don't give it the chance to speak. I become even more self-affirming, telling myself: **I will win! I can be the best! I can achieve whatever I put my mind to!**

STOP "SHOULDING" ON YOURSELF

"SHOULDS" AND "OUGHT TOS" ARE THE GREAT GUILT TRIPS WE put on ourselves. They can cause so much unnecessary pain and agony throughout life. And they are a difficult voice to eliminate. Almost from the day we learned to speak, our parents were telling us what we should or shouldn't be doing. If we didn't live up to those commands, we experienced guilt or an internal sense of shame.

I admit this is a difficult category, because some of the "I should" statements we received in childhood seemed appropriate. "You should be kind to others," our parents would say. Nothing wrong about that, right? Of course not. But an emotion like kindness works best because we *want* to be kind, not because we think we *should* be. Our greatest, most positive action derives from our own desire, not from a voice of guilt telling us this is what we ought to be doing.

Years ago, I realized I was doing good things for the wrong reasons. I was being generous and considerate because I thought I should be, not because of the joy such behavior now brings me. What had been left out of my actions was the factor of personal choice. I still heard a subtle voice saying that I was not in control of my life. As a result, my goodness was not empowering. **My negative voice was still overriding my good deeds.**

So here's what I did. I began to pay close attention to my language to hear how many "shoulds" and "ought tos" I had been putting on myself. Each time it happened, I would stop and ask myself, "Why *should* I do this?" I then made myself decide whether I would participate in a certain behavior or not. If I did, I gave myself the credit for making the decision. I said, "I choose to do the following!" As a result, I felt a sense of positive self-esteem that I never had felt before. I also realized that some of the things I had been doing because I had thought I "should" be doing them were inappropriate for my current life. For example, after reevaluating my "shoulds," I decided to change churches because I knew such a decision would be better for my life. Previously, I had been staying at my old church because I thought I "should" stay in the denomination rather than going where I felt spiritually renewed. The more I took personal responsibility for my life, the more successful I felt.

"I WISH" IS A COP-OUT

ALMOST EVERY DAY, WE SAY SOMETHING TO OURSELVES LIKE "I wish I had more money," "I wish I could lose ten pounds," "I wish I could take a vacation," or "I wish I could find someone to share my life with." Ah, wishful thinking! Wishes provide us with only a false, temporary feeling that we are focusing on our goals. Wishing gives up control of the situation! When we "wish," we are not taking responsibility for our lives, and we are not taking significant steps toward growth.

Anybody can wish for something. I used to be addicted to wishing. Then I realized there is a difference between a word like "will" and words like "wish," "want," or "hope." There is a huge difference between the sentences "I wish I were happy," "I want to be happy," and "I am willing to change my life so that I become happy." Only the last statement leads one to change.

When I stopped wishing, I gave control back to me—to change whatever it was that I wanted or chose to change.

WHY ASK WHY?

As I HAVE SAID BEFORE, IT IS IMPORTANT FOR US TO ASK QUESTIONS about the negative attitudes that flow through our lives. Yet beware: Such questioning will take us only so far. Too many of us get caught up in the trap of searching for deeper meanings. Urged on by pop psychology books—by now, I think I've read a hundred—we can spend our time digging into the causes of our negative voices. We do that for one simple reason: it's our way of feeling as if we're doing something while still avoiding change. Rather than developing our own solid techniques to get rid of our negative voices, we seem content merely to read about our negative voices and question where they came from.

I have learned the hard way that when it comes to negative voices, actions speak louder than words. I confess, I spent years dillydallying with my life on this long, supposedly intellectual search as I asked myself, over and over, "Why do I have these negative voices? Why do I give myself such negative labels?" **But I didn't spend any of that time trying to change my behavior!** In truth, continuing to ask the "why" questions—"Why do I feel so incapable?" "Why am I scared to follow my heart?" "Why won't I try harder to lose weight?"—ensured that I would keep following my negative voice and keep hanging on to whatever it was I was questioning.

After a long process of trial and error, I learned that getting the negative voices out of my head didn't require huge insight. I just had to do it! It's simply a conscious choice! In fact, several studies by behavioral psychologists have shown that it's after we make significant changes that we are able to get insight into why we have been burdened by those negative voices.

Here's an exercise for you. Pick what could be considered a mundane problem in your life—it could be something as minor as your inability to get up when you want in the morning. Without even attempting to figure out why you have a negative voice that wants you to stay in bed and not face the day, promise yourself that you will spend the next two weeks changing the behavior that troubles you. When your negative voice emerges ("I should have gotten up." "I'm just lazy!"), don't waste time wondering where it comes from. Just replace it with a positive message ("Let's get ready for a great day!"), and move forward.

If you're anything like me, you'll realize that the change in behavior is far more exciting than understanding every detail about why the behavior existed in the first place.

LET GO OF NEGATIVE IMAGES

ONE OF MY GREAT CHALLENGES IN LIFE IS NOT TO GET OBSESSIVE over my setbacks. In the past, I have been a terror. What would be a wonderful day to someone else would be a complete failure to me because of a single brief conversation that didn't turn out right or a remark made by someone that I would take personally. Days would pass, and I would still get upset over a minor slight that had happened to me the previous week.

If we're not prepared, unhappy thoughts will come into our heads at the strangest times for absolutely no reason whatsoever. They often happen to us in the car when we're driving to or from work. They happen when we're taking a shower. They happen during peaceful times, like right before we go to bed.

Is there anything to be learned from these moments? For years, I was convinced there was something to be discovered from such down periods. But there's a lot more to be learned from an old phrase, "Let go and let God." Indeed, there is little to be learned when thoughts come creeping back into your head about the argument you had with a friend or neighbor last month. There is no reward in those memories about an unpleasant scene with a relative. If we let them, those negative moments only breed more negatives, leading to deeper, disheartening thoughts and anxieties.

Have you ever been in a position where you felt nearly paralyzed by a negative image? Have you ever carried on an imaginary conversation with someone you resent—even though you know it doesn't help anything? You tell yourself to shift gears, to stop this imaginary conversation, yet it keeps going. Why?

It's because we don't know how to let the positive parts of our brain overcome our negative parts. The key to getting rid of a negative image is to "divert" our brain from that image the moment it shows up. Some people are able to say, "Go away, negative image!"—and it does. But most of us need a tool to break the disempowering thought patterns that we are in.

This chapter started with the title "A Clean Windshield." Think of that as clear vision. When a negative thought comes to mind, clean the windshield!

Think about wiping away the negative thought. Visualize cleaning your windows (or thoughts) with a soft, clean cloth that wipes them away!

Now, with a clean view of the real world, think about what you see around you. Go back to the negative thought and turn it around. Example—negative: "I've never completed a goal like this before." Positive: "I'm capable of achieving whatever I choose. This is a new goal and I'm working toward it." Now you have cleaned your windshield and prepared your subconscious for success.

Here's a second technique. Keep photographs with you of the people most precious to you—family, friends, a beloved pet, cherished relatives who have passed away, or even a picture of you at your favorite vacation spot. When a negative image comes in, look at those pictures to remind yourself of what you do have and how much there is to be thankful for.

The End of the Negative Thought

FOR ME, THERE IS A GREAT RELEASE IN THE SIMPLE EXERCISE of replacing my negative voices and images with positive ones. The more I do these exercises, the more I realize that the negative voices inside me are not my own. They are the result of years of conditioning. As my own words and visions become more positive, then the negative voices fade away.

The same will happen to you. There is plenty of evidence to suggest that revoicing our attitudes and our feelings will have an enormous influence over our lives. What we say about ourselves goes a long way in determining the outcome of our journey. It is a powerful strategy to get ourselves going on the right road—and, most important, to stay committed to that road. You will develop the kind of love and respect for yourself that you never before had. You will be thrilled at the opportunity to communicate with yourself in healthy ways.

So prepare yourself. Seek out your true voice. Let it fill

your head with positive inner images that can protect and inspire you. And, like a warrior, slay any thought that is not designed to make you a winner.

We are the masters of our thoughts. We can control our thoughts. And with practice and discipline, we can turn those thoughts into positive action and create a personal destiny second to none.

III

Your Road Map for Life

Rediscovering Your Own Hopes and Dreams

There's no one else in the world who can do what you can do,
who can think and see the way you do, who can create what you
can create. Our dreams are those things that make us unique.
They give us a purpose. They allow us to feel authentic.

It's Your Road

Deciding What You Want for Yourself

If we don't go after our own dreams, we've lost an invaluable treasure. We will find ourselves leading a life without challenges or aspirations. Life is too precious to get caught on a road that someone else chose for us without our even knowing it.

BY THIS POINT IN THE BOOK, WE'RE LEARNING TO LOVE OURselves again. We're understanding why it's healthy to shut down the negative voices in our head and replace them with positive ones. We're learning to turn our positive thinking into positive action. We're starting to touch that glorious part inside us that is so full of life and creativity.

We're overhauling our engines—our inner selves. Now it's time to have some fun. **Let's push down on the accelerator!**

Right now, we are in the position of taking our rediscovered belief in ourselves and letting it carry us anywhere we want to go in life. We are ready to accomplish anything we want, whether it is to start a new career, advance ourselves in the careers we already have, develop deeper and more intimate relationships with our spouses, friends, or children, or even do such things as stop smoking or lose weight and keep it off!

We can do it! **We can do whatever we choose!**

Forgetting Your Road Map

U H-OH. TIME OUT. I HAVE A FEELING YOU MAY BE GETting anxious. You may be wanting to raise your hand and say: "But, Jinger, I don't know exactly what it is that I want."

It's a little frustrating knowing you have this great car with a powerful engine but not knowing exactly where to direct it. Maybe you're ready to tear off down the road, but you don't have a road map to guide you.

Believe me, you're not the only person who's thought this way. All of us have asked the question "What do I want to do with my life?" I think that's a major reason the world is so full of frustrated people. They know they have great potential, but, tragically, they have not taken the time to figure out in which direction to head. They have not created a vision of what they want to do with themselves. It is not that they don't want to change, but they cannot imagine what to change into. The writer Gertrude Stein put it more succinctly. On her deathbed, when she was asked, "What's the answer?," her response was "What's the question?"

There are so many of us who remain unfocused about our

goals throughout our lifetime. We follow roads in whatever direction those roads happen to be going. Because we don't know where to turn, we settle for what is available. Sometimes, if an opportunity is laid before us, we'll take it. Yet many of us fail to decide to *create* opportunities for ourselves.

Eventually, we may realize we are on a road to nowhere— but we don't pull off to the side and study our map in order to change roads. In our lives, some of us meander from one thing to another, rarely taking an inventory of our abilities, not working at finding out what our true desires are. We go through life doing what we think we're *supposed* to be doing—being a good wife, or keeping a tidy home, or having a good career. Please understand me. All of those goals are great—as long as they are what *you* want! But some of us are doing nothing more than following some silent message we have been receiving all of our lives: the message of expectation. We are expected to go along with the norm and do the socially accepted thing in order to avoid rocking the boat.

I will never forget asking a friend of mine how she would sum up her life. She said one word: "Regret." It was an astonishing answer. By any standard, she had lived well. She had a good husband, she had created a home for him and their children, and she did plenty of volunteer and charity work to raise funds for great causes.

"What is missing?" I asked.

She looked at me. "Jinger, I really don't know what I want," she said. "But I know I haven't gotten it."

So many of us are in that very position, feeling liked caged birds but not sure how to unlock the door. For years, psychologists and psychiatrists have claimed that their patients showed one major symptom: they were unable to say clearly what they wanted to do to change themselves. A lot of research shows that people are unhappy in their jobs—not because they aren't making enough money, but because they don't know what to do instead.

And that includes those people who are in highly successful careers. Those of you who have been in fast-track jobs know very well that it's not everything that it's said to be. You jet-set, you make a great salary, and you receive admiration and respect from other people. Indeed, you've got the success everybody thinks they want, too. You look as if you're not only on the right road, but you're on a superhighway, racing at top speed in a sexy little sports car.

All of which makes it harder for you to ask, "Is this what I want? Is this what I want my real life's work to be?"

Once again, for some, such a life is exactly what they want—and more power to them. Others might discover, however, that they are unable to balance their career and personal life in a way that makes them happy. They not only don't have time to eat a leisurely meal with their families, but they also don't have time to cook it. Some of us don't have the time to find a mate so we can have a family in the first place.

A very competent, financially successful woman named Anne once told me that she regularly dreamed she was racing from one place to another—from a business lunch to a board meeting to a shopping boutique—and no matter where she went, she would ask whomever she saw, "Have you seen Anne?" In the dream, each person she approached told her the same thing. "Oh, you must have just missed her. She was here a minute ago." And Anne would move to the next location.

"It was a nightmare," Anne told me. "I could never catch up with myself."

In other words, she didn't know what she wanted, and the

way she handled it was by going faster and faster. Just as there are some of us who have had trouble getting up to speed in our lives, so there are some of us who have trouble slowing down!

Real Dreams Versus Unreal Dreams

WE ALL HAVE TO LIVE WITH TRADE-OFFS. PART OF LIFE is not doing everything we wish to do. But we can make our lives special by making sure that we never lose focus on the one or two things that we really want. I admit, this is hard to do. In our high-tech, information-age culture, which is characterized by financial pressures and frantic hurry-up attitudes, it is easy to become overwhelmed. We toil on in our jobs without satisfaction—jobs that can be so stressful that there seems to be nothing left over for the rest of our lives. Or we race like mad to feed our kids and get them to school. We sit down at lunch and flip through a magazine, stare at a pretty woman in an advertisement, and we think, "Gosh, when do I have the time for me anymore?"

Indeed, we can feel completely burdened just trying to get through a day. No wonder so many of us are still waiting for someone to come to us with a glass slipper that will magically change our lives.

I have good news for you. We can create the magic for ourselves. We can create the life we want. **We can reach beyond our limits and invest our lives with meaning.**

Real dreams aren't unrealistic at all. Notice that I said "real dreams." There is a difference between "real" dreams and "escapist" dreams. An escapist dream would be abandoning your family and moving to Tahiti to become a beach bum, or marrying a movie star who meets you on an airplane. That is a fantasy. But a real dream is something that makes your heart sing. It could be anything from going back to school to starting your own small business to entering the corporate world. It could be writing your first book. It could be finding a way to make money part-time so you could start saving for the glorious vacation you have always wanted to take. It could be making the effort to meet the kind of man you would want to live with for the rest of your life. Maybe you've always wanted to work with underprivileged people. It could mean moving your family from a big city to a Norman Rockwell–like small town.

Your dream is that thing which you feel is uniquely yours. It is what makes you feel authentic. It is what makes you believe you have a purpose. It is what makes your life light up.

Is that happening in your life? If you're unhappy—if you feel a sense of dissatisfaction—then recognize that your heart is sending you a message. It's telling you to stop listening to those voices clamoring in your head about everything that you *should* be doing. It's telling you to do what you *want* to do for yourself. Your heart is not telling you to abandon everything else. But it's reminding you that if you forget your inner spirit and your deepest desires, then you will never know the thrilling possibility of success.

Winners in life are those who know exactly what they want and who are on the road to obtaining it. It's as simple as that. In the 1980s, two Harvard psychologists did a study of people who considered themselves happy. They found that what these people had in common was not money or good health or a loving romantic relationship. What they had in common was that they knew what they wanted and they felt they were moving in the right direction to get it. That's what made life feel great. They were headed for something they loved. As the old saying goes, "Once you find what you truly love doing, you will never have to work another day in your life."

It's true. Unless you are doing what you want to do, it doesn't matter how many nice things you have or what kind of car you drive or how big your home is. No one has invented the material object that can make up for the loss of an unfulfilled life.

It's not too late. **We can choose to go after what we want!** We can create our life like a work of art—putting the colors and shapes on the canvas ourselves, creating the self-portrait we want. No matter what kind of position we are in—no matter how old or how poor or how unhappy or how beaten down we think we are—our portrait is still waiting patiently for us to finish it. And we have the power to complete it! As I like to say, "This is the day your dreams can come true. What the mind can conceive and believe, it can achieve!"

Setting Yourself Free

SO NOW IT IS TIME FOR US TO ASK OURSELVES, AS WE HAVE never asked before: What do we really want out of life? What are our real dreams and how do we plan to achieve them?

When it comes to dreams, nobody is going to make us fulfill them. If we never write that novel or take our dream vacation or start our business, nobody is going to care. Nobody else is going to push us. It's up to us alone to be the author of our own destiny. We must write our own life story. We are responsible for our success.

If that sounds scary, just recall how far we have come since we opened this book. We have recovered that wonderful and loving positive side within us. We know we can overcome any negative voice. We know we have the inner strength to drive down whatever road we choose, to live by our own dreams, not the dreams chosen for us by someone else. And it's never, ever too late to get started. History is dotted with women who made their marks late in life. At age fifty-three, Margaret Thatcher became Britain's first female prime minister. At seventy-one, Golda Meir became prime minister of Israel. At eighty, Grandma Moses, who had started painting in her late seventies, had her first one-woman exhibit.

Am I suggesting that you become a world-famous politician or artist? Maybe! But in our own ways, we can do exactly what those women have done. I could tell you hundreds of stories about women in our company who first came to us feeling as if they had been drifting through life, letting others define who they were. They weren't such high-spirited go-getters when I first met them. They were women who weren't sure what their options were, who felt their hopes for a more exciting future were futile.

Remember Cheryl, the woman who told me she no longer knew if she had any dreams? When I met her, she was like so many other women I had met before—completely down on herself psychologically, feeling so inadequate, thinking the only thing she was good at doing was caring for others, such as her husband and her children. During the day, she said, she'd sit at home, watching television, too intimidated to even call a friend for lunch because she didn't want anyone to see how empty her life was.

"So why are you here?" I asked.

"Jinger," she told me, "I've got about a third of my life to live, and I want to prove that I'm good at something. I've always thought I was good at working with people. And now I'm going to try."

With that one comment, she had begun to turn her car toward the right road. That's all it took. It was a very small step: in her spare time, she was going to work out of her home selling our products. She was not on her way to becoming prime minister. But because Cheryl finally had decided to do something she wanted, she had begun to empower her own life. The more her self-esteem grew, the more minor her problems were. What Cheryl learned was that it's impossible to feel depressed about yourself for a very long period of time if you are moving toward your dreams. People who move forward behave in positive, successful ways. Those who have belief in their personal worth become magnets for success and happiness. Good things drop into their laps regularly, their dreams are usually carried to completion, and they have a way of enjoying the pleasures that the day brings. And it's all because they are "driving" to create opportunities for themselves!

In fact, because Cheryl made the decision to believe in herself, she began to develop skills she didn't know she had. She soon found herself capable of selling just about anything to anybody, managing large groups of people, advancing quickly in her career, making large amounts of money—and still working out of her own home (which, today, is a dream home that she has built from her own earnings).

I call her story a modern parable, because there are so many stories like hers—women making dramatic changes despite the odds against them. I also can't help but think of my and my husband Dick's own story when we started our business. Despite every so-called expert telling us our venture would not work, we discovered that there's real power in going for what you want—in truly making the effort to fulfill your dreams.

The power of our dreams can set us free. There's no one else in the world who can do what you can do, who can think and see the way you do, who can create what you can create. As one philosopher from ancient days wrote, "The universe is not going to see someone like you again in the entire history of creation."

If we don't go after our dreams, we've lost an invaluable treasure. We will find ourselves leading a life without challenges or aspirations. Life is too precious to get caught on a road that someone else chose for us without our even knowing it. That is practically a guarantee that our road will be paved with mediocrity or unhappiness.

So let's move on. As you're about to find out, there are some simple, effective ways to focus on and follow your dreams—and make them happen!

Mission Possible!

A Personal Mission Statement to Guide Your Journey

Whenever we feel things in our lives are foggy, our Personal Mission Statement can be like automobile headlights, illuminating our destination. We will find it much easier to recognize which steps we need to take to get to where we want to go. We will let nothing get in the way of turning our desires into reality.

ONE OF THE MOST POPULAR SERVICES AT OUR COMPANY IS A FREE computerized image analysis that we call the Personal Image Profile. Our customers answer a series of questions about everything from their facial shape to their tastes in fashion in order to discover their fashion personality. As part of our services, we also provide a free "color analysis," which helps customers choose the right colors for their skin tone, as well as a patented "skin condition analysis" to determine their skin type.

Our theory is very simple: We cannot come up with an effective and lasting "cosmetics makeover" for our customers unless we do some solid research about them. In the same way, you cannot come up with a lifelong "inner makeover" unless you know exactly what your goals in life are.

Because many women I meet feel like Cheryl—women who believe they have lived mostly unfulfilled lives—it is hard for them initially to say what it is they truly want to do with their lives. While they might not consciously know what they *want*, they've been through enough setbacks to know what they *don't want*. So I tell them to start there. I tell them to get a pen and a sheet of paper and make a list of everything they don't want.

When we set out to discover what we want, we first must be absolutely clear what we do *not* want.

So many of us don't realize this, but it's a vital step. In creating our new future, we must be adamant that this future doesn't include the things we dislike from the past. Sure, we can't get rid of all of life's little hassles—doing the laundry is an example that comes to mind—but if there is some time-consuming activity in our lives that fills us with dread, then we have the power not to do it.

So as part of our plan to discover what we truly want, here is our first exercise. **Write down what you don't want.** Write down anything that comes to mind, and don't worry about the significance of it—and don't worry if it sounds self-indulgent. If you dislike visiting your in-laws, put it down. If you dislike keeping a checkbook, put it down. If you are filled with unhappiness when you think about your job, put it down. If you hate to shop, put it down. Remember, the point of living is to find the things that make our hearts sing!

Step 1.
Ten Things I Do Not Want to Do

1. _____

2. _____

3. _____

4. _____

5. _____

6. _____

7. _____

8. _____

9. _____

10. _____

If you have come up with more than ten, no problem. But, now, study your list and rate each one. Come up with the three or four things you most dislike to do—and you're well on your way to understanding what you long for. For example, I listed "unstructured days" as something I disliked. While I relish free time at the end of the day and on weekends to restore my batteries, I simply dislike periods during Mondays through Fridays when I have no particular focus. I am so schedule-oriented during the weekdays that I even like to have my "recreation time" or "family time" plugged into my calendar.

Now try this. Take three or four items you wrote down as things you don't want, and write down their opposites! For example, if you wrote down "taking orders" as something you don't want, then the opposite might be "becoming my own boss." Or if you dislike an activity, then write down what you would prefer doing instead of that activity. If you dislike cooking dinner—and, hey, let's face it, at the end of a workday, a lot of working women can barely tolerate the idea of coming home to cook—then write down your preference. It might be reading poetry. It might be going to a late-afternoon aerobics class. It might be sitting on the couch watching the evening news.

Do you see what you're doing? You're beginning to realize what your desires are. If you really dislike cooking dinner, then fine. Start asking yourself, "What is something I can do to keep me from doing what I dislike? Is it to hire some help in the afternoon who will cook dinner before he or she leaves? Is it to arrange to have more meals delivered to your home and learn not to feel guilty about it?" Already, your mind is contemplating answers—it is not still stuck on problems.

Step 2.
Ten Experiences I Would Like to Have

SOMETIMES, WHEN I ASK PEOPLE WHAT THEY WANT IN LIFE, THEY usually tell me something like "A new home." There's nothing wrong with a new home, of course—as long as you understand why you want it. Part of becoming a complete person is recognizing the emotions that drive our desires. If one of your desires, for instance, is to become very wealthy, then ask yourself what you believe is the underlying emotional need for that money. Is it security? Peace of mind? Public recognition?

That's what you're going to do in this exercise. You're going to start exploring what particular "quality of life" you want for yourself. What "emotional" experiences do you want to have? Try not to think of this exercise in terms of material items, but simply in terms of *mindfulness* such as serenity, connection with God, desire to lead others, and so on.

1. _____

2. _____

3. _____

4. _____

5. _____

6. _____

7. _____

8. _____

9. _____

10. _____

Step 3.
Ten Ways to Improve My Emotional Well-Being

Now, we're getting closer to understanding what we want. Look again at the emotions that you listed in Step 2 and pick one that feels especially important to you. It could be "peace of mind" or "loving relationship." Now here's the chance to get specific. Again, be as self-indulgent as you want. List ten things that you believe will help you obtain that emotional feeling. You might come up with more than ten, which is fine. You might come up with what seem like strange answers. Again, that's fine. No one is going to read this but you.

1. _____

2. _____

3. _____

4. _____

5. _____

6. _____

7. _____

8. _____

9. _____

10. _____

Step 4.
Ten Unimportant Things I Enjoy Doing

LET'S NOW MOVE FROM THE IMPORTANT EMOTIONS TO SEEMINGLY ordinary things. It's important that you identify even the smallest things you enjoy doing. So if you really enjoy having a cup of coffee alone each morning after everyone has left the house, put it down. If you find great pleasure in pulling weeds from a flower bed, put that down, too.

1. _____

2. _____

3. _____

4. _____

5. _____

6. _____

7. _____

8. _____

9. _____

10. _____

Step 5.
Ten Specific Activities I Might Like to Do

IN THIS STEP, I'M NOT ASKING FOR A MAJOR COMMITMENT. I'M not asking you to stand up and say, "This is what I'm going to become for the rest of my life!" I'm simply asking you to daydream. Be tentative, if you wish. If you think you'd like to be an astronomer, but you can't imagine how you could get the education to do that, don't be concerned. Just write it down. And stay specific. In other words, if you think you might like to travel more often, put down where you want to go, such as "Live in the South of France for a summer." Don't just write "Travel."

1. _____

2. _____

3. _____

4. _____

5. _____

6. _____

7. _____

8. _____

9. _____

10. _____

Step 6.
More Exercises to Help You Find What You Want

UNCOVERING OUR HIDDEN DREAMS AND DESIRES IS NOT ALWAYS an easy process. Sometimes, we need to reexamine ourselves to understand what we truly want.

If you feel stuck, or a little uncertain about your desires, try these exercises.

1. Read biographies or autobiographies of famous people you admire. I love to read about those who have come out of nowhere to do something with their lives. By reading about the way these people decided to direct their lives, we can get ideas about how to direct ours to make an impact. We can learn how great people live. Their stories are not only inspirational, they have the ability to show us how to build our own futures. Look through the "Biography" or "Nonfiction" shelves of a bookstore, and you are certain to find something that appeals to you.

2. Write your own autobiography. It is amazing what happens when people start writing down little episodes about their earlier years. I'm talking about our preteen and teen years, when we were so idealistic and full of hopes and dreams. Usually, we lose touch with this part of ourselves as we get older. Writing about these moments is often healing, exciting, and motivating. They remind us of the best parts of ourselves.

3. Keep a journal. Sometimes, we get so caught up in the dailiness of life that we forget to take time to know what we really like and what we really dislike about ourselves. "Journaling" helps us get more in touch with our feelings. The simple act of writing down our reactions to events of the day helps increase our self-awareness, and thus helps us recognize what we really want. Even a few sentences is fine!

4. Write a story about your imaginary twin. This is a great exercise often used by psychologists in which you pretend you have a twin, one who looks and acts just like you. Now imagine her having the ideal life. Would she have a different lifestyle? Would she be more free-spirited? Would she work in the same job? Would she have stayed home so often? Would she have different friends? What places would she have seen? Where would she be today? Do you see what you're doing? By writing a story about this twin of yours, you are writing about your own hopes and dreams.

5. Write your own eulogy. Here's another way to discover your deepest ambitions. Imagine the person who is giving your eulogy at your own funeral. This person is going to detail your accomplishments and personality attributes. How do you want the eulogy to read? It's your chance to have anything that you want said about you. Do you want to be known as the most positive person people have ever known? The kindest person? The most peaceful? This will help you formulate your goals.

6. Write down your dreams at night. Sound strange? Actually, throughout history, dreams have been used to unlock inner knowledge. Ancient kings had dream interpreters. Sigmund Freud claimed that dreams were the "royal road to the unconscious mind." And psychiatrists today are trained to study their clients' dreams for tips about their deepest desires. We dream up to two hours each night, which for most of us will add up to spending six years in the dream state. Considering that authors and visual artists regularly use dreams for their creative inspiration, why don't we do the same thing?

I'm not saying that our dreams will tell us exactly what we must do in life. But dreams are another way for us to reach a deeper level of awareness. We are giving our unconscious the chance to speak directly to us and develop us in ways we haven't thus far. Dreams give us energy and enthusiasm, and they allow us to come up with creative solutions to our problems. Most significantly, they can inspire us to see a future that is better than the present. As we'll discuss more in the next chapter, what our unconscious selves can imagine can readily be transformed to our conscious minds.

Perhaps you think you do not dream at all. But research proves we are dreaming while asleep every ninety minutes or so. We just haven't made the effort to remember our dreams. A good tool to help remember dreams is a "dream journal," or a pad (and flashlight!), that you can keep beside your bed so you can write down any dreams you remember the moment you awaken. The more you do this, the more you train your mind to remember your dreams. It's also helpful, before going to sleep, for you to remind yourself that you want to remember your dreams.

If there is an issue that is bothering you, you can do what is called "dream seeding," in which you actually write down a question you want to have addressed in your dream. Some people put the question under their pillow before going to sleep. They might write, "Where do I want to go with my life?" Then, they think about that question before drifting off to sleep. While it may take us a few nights before we clearly remember our dreams, it will happen! We will feel empowered, as if we have found a mentor who is there to help us while our eyes are closed. Our dreams will help us gain deeper insights into our fears, our needs, and our goals.

As far as interpreting dreams, we don't always need a professionally trained analyst to help us. Many dreams are easily decipherable—we usually dream either about people or situations already in our lives, or people or situations that we *want* in our lives. One way to think of our dreaming is that it is like a jigsaw puzzle. The pieces of that puzzle might include "self," "work," "conflict," "play," "kids," "husband," and so on. If we dream for several nights in a row about one of those pieces, such as a "conflict" in our lives, then we probably know that there's something in our conscious life that could use some work.

Step 7.
Study What You've Written

SOMEWHERE ON YOUR LISTS IN STEPS 1 THROUGH 6 ARE THE clues to what really makes your heart sing. Your daydreams are there, your favorite activities are listed, you've fantasized about yourself, and you've even written down little details that make you smile during the day. All in all, your future is on these pages. At the least, you may be surprised at how much you've written down. You probably thought you had no idea what you wanted, remember?

Study your lists, your autobiography, your eulogy, and your dream writing. Add to them or subtract, if you want. Once again, these are only exercises to help you focus. You might change your lists tomorrow. They merely are a way for you to do some creative exploring, to check out your interests, and to try different experiences in your mind. Pay careful attention to anything that excites you—even a little.

Now, after studying your lists, condense the five most appealing images from Steps 1 through 5 and list them below. They don't have to be in any order; nor do you have to list only your most far-reaching or significant wants. Feel free to include the unimportant things. But make sure these are the things that appeal to you most.

1. _____

2. _____

3. _____

4. _____

5. _____

Step 8.
Create a Personal Mission Statement

NOW IT'S TIME TO START DEVELOPING A MORE DETAILED ROAD map so we can move from our theories and wish lists into the real world. And I know no better way to start that road map than for us to write out our own "mission statement."*

Mission statements are used in business all the time. A corporation lays out a set of guiding principles that clearly state its philosophy and its goals. Our company's mission statement, for example, is "to offer women a lifetime of self-confidence through products and services designed to enhance their personal appearance . . . and within a nurturing environment, provide women with a rewarding full-time or part-time earnings opportunity limited only by their initiative."

It's a wonderful tool for us. Whenever we get into big policy-making meetings, and we wonder if a new plan is what we want, we will pull out our mission statement and read it. As simple as it is, our corporate mission statement reminds us precisely what matters most to our company. And that's exactly what a Personal Mission Statement can do. It is there to help us make sure we are headed in the direction we want to go.

Perhaps you noticed that our business's mission statement didn't say anything like "We want to earn 'x' millions each year" or "We hope to be really well known someday." Our corporate statement involves principles that we hope will govern the rest of our business lives. In the same way, our Personal Mission Statement must embody our deepest val-

---

* For further discussion of Personal Mission Statements, please see Stephen R. Covey's *The 7 Habits of Highly Effective People* (Fireside, 1990).

ues. It is there to remind us that if we try to be the best we can be as human beings, then everything else—success, financial rewards, happiness, and so on—will follow.

Now, look over the lists you've made and your writing. This time, look especially for the quality that seems to underlie everything you want to be. Perhaps you want to be a great, powerful leader; perhaps you want to be a doctor; perhaps you want to get involved in a career for the first time in your life in order to prove to yourself and others that you can make money on your own; perhaps you want to get your Ph.D.; perhaps you want to run a charity ball; perhaps you want to get into super athletic shape; perhaps you want to learn how to speed-read two thousand words per minute so you can read more books; perhaps you want to save $30,000 in the next few years to start a college fund for your children; perhaps you want to learn a foreign language.

Whatever your desire is: Great! Remember what I said in the introduction to this book? No dream you cherish is too grand or too insignificant. No arena you strive to excel in is too large or too small.

Your Personal Mission Statement is designed for you to emphasize the underlying reason that you want to change. If you want to become a doctor, then maybe it is because your deepest desire is to help others. If you want to become a leader, then maybe it is because your deepest desire is to develop your character to the fullest.

Here's a great example that came from one of our saleswomen: **"My mission in life is not only to attain a state of vibrant physical health that allows me to feel confident and attractive in front of others, but also to develop an equally attractive state of emotional well-being that lets me live with integrity, honor, and kindness to others. My mission is to live my**

life with great joy and to display the kind of energy that will bring me friends, happiness, and financial success."

Now it's your turn. Again, I want to remind you that this is not a test. Don't worry if it sounds too vague. You can refine this statement over the next weeks and months as often as you want. Moreover, your Personal Mission Statement does not demand perfection; it only has to ask for improvement over your current status.

Personal Mission Statement

_____

_____

_____

_____

_____

_____

Congratulations! You now have a beacon that will keep you on course and prevent you from exiting onto the wrong road. In the future if you feel confused or lost, all you have to do is read your Personal Mission Statement.

Indeed, simply by having a mission—and by training our

minds to concentrate on successfully completing that mission—we are one step closer to creating a truly unshakable belief that every single one of our dreams can come true. Have you ever studied real winners in life and wondered why they seem to do all the right things at becoming more successful? It's because they are focused on their missions. They are geared toward attaining their goals. They don't think about the negatives. They expect success!

Whenever we feel things in our lives are foggy, our Personal Mission Statement can be like automobile headlights, illuminating our destination. We will find it much easier to recognize which steps we need to take to get to where we have to. We will let nothing get in the way of turning our desires into reality. Indeed, if we let our Personal Mission Statement permeate our life, we will discover over time that our mind automatically knows what is good for us and what is not.

We will find it much easier to recognize which steps we need to take next to move up the ladder of success. We will instinctively begin to see the areas in which we need to concentrate. We will no longer have to guess at what to do. We will find ourselves getting breaks that we never could have planned for, because we never knew those breaks existed in the first place. Just by having a Personal Mission Statement, our attitudes about ourselves and our capabilities will change.

Now let's turn the page and develop some strategies to make sure our Personal Mission Statements come true. It's time to set goals!

9

Goals to Keep You Going

Breaking Down Your Journey into Steps for Success

It has been said that goals are like magnets. They constantly pull
us toward them. Once we give ourselves goals and set
ourselves firmly on the path of meeting them, our lives
will change dramatically.

HAVE YOU EVER HEARD THE OLD SAYING "IF YOU AIM AT NOTH-
ing, you'll hit it"? Have you ever had one of those Saturdays
in which you wake up with no plans and you find yourself
accomplishing next to nothing, aimlessly drifting through
the day?

Although the Personal Mission Statement we just completed is one of the most important things we can do for

ourselves, our mission will be fruitless if we do not set precise goals to accomplish. If we want our lives to change—if we want to be doing something completely different ten years from now, for example—we cannot sit around and wait, and *then* start creating that life in ten years.

We must have a clear plan within which we know that we are constantly advancing in the direction of our ultimate destination. And we have to start this very day setting goals to get there.

Goal setting! Does that sound like an old cliché to you?

Well, it's been used for a long time, but it sure does work. When Dick and I said we were going to start our own business, other people said we were crazy. They thought we had lost our minds when we told them that we were taking out a $600,000 loan in order to create a company that we said would change the lives of women throughout America. What did we know about building a major corporation? they asked. Dick had been a successful executive, but he had never built his own business before. I had very little business knowledge. I had been spending my days as a wife and mother, periodically taking on a client or two to help them with interior design.

But instead of being overwhelmed at the audacity of our plan, Dick and I sat down, wrote our mission statement, and then came up with some very clear goals about building our company into a success. We set goals for sales, for the recruitment of saleswomen, and for the improvement of our products. We established short-term goals to get us through each week, and we came up with long-term goals to ensure profitability within three years. We wanted this company to become the world's premier skin care and image company. In fact, we were so bold as to make that goal our corporate slogan: "The World's Premier Skin Care and Image Company."

Why would we set such a goal for ourselves? Well, why

not? As I've said before, it takes no more energy to dream big than it does to dream small. We knew that we could turn our business into such a company as long as we continued to believe in ourselves. We didn't care who laughed at us.

What we did is absolutely no different from what you can do for your own life's project. We defined our mission, we set our goals, we rolled up our sleeves, and we went to work. Admittedly, for the first couple of years, we were flat broke, and at times we came close to losing the company because we could not pay back our loans. We had to take out new loans, find new investors, and hang on.

But we kept reviewing our goals—and sticking to them! We knew that as long as we were on the right track, we would become a success. We personally interviewed prospective saleswomen, we introduced new lines of products, and we believed! The secret to our success was that we had drive and a conviction that we could do whatever we set out to do. That's it.

And sure enough, our sales went from $761,000 in 1981 to over $30 million retail in 1985. The company's sales have been expanding ever since. And, most important, tens of thousands of women have learned to believe in themselves enough to start their own home-based businesses that have earned millions for some of them.

That kind of result is a testament to the power of goal setting!

Goals are like magnets. They constantly pull us toward them. Once we give ourselves goals and set ourselves firmly on the path of meeting them, our lives will change dramatically. And as we reach each goal, we will discover that we have even more goals we want to accomplish. We will wake up every day feeling a passion to get even more things accomplished. We will feel productive and confident in a way we never knew we could feel. We will develop far more control over our destiny. I guarantee you that goals are a great key to teach us to believe in ourselves—and with such belief, we will realize that nothing is impossible!

The Risk of Setting a Goal

Y OU MIGHT FEEL A LITTLE SILLY AS YOU BEGIN THE PROCESS of setting specific goals for your life. Other people might laugh at you, as they did at Dick and me.

When we set goals for ourselves, we are taking on a major risk—because we are having to get very specific with ourselves about our desires. I remember telling our research staff that I wanted to invent something that would keep a bra strap from slipping. "Maybe some kind of glue for your bra," I said. Everyone laughed. The whole company thought it was my nuttiest idea. But I said, "Guys, when you finish laughing, let's get to work. We're going to call it BodyGlue and it is my goal to have it on the market by the end of the year." When we did introduce BodyGlue, major fashion magazines praised it, and when I personally introduced it on the QVC shopping channel, we sold fifteen thousand units in twelve minutes!

Believe me, as you set your goals, other people are going to tell you, "Don't take risks," "You'll be better off if you play it safe," "You might fail if you try." Frankly, I can't think of any worse advice, for there is nothing more glorious than getting off the safe road of mediocrity. It's these individuals who dare to venture who enjoy the most satisfaction, who do the most good for other people, who experience the greatest happiness, and who make the most money. According to one report, 80 percent of today's millionaires came from families of poor or only modest means. When a research foundation conducted a major study to determine what it takes to become a successful executive—interview-

ing leaders in business, government, science, and religion—
it discovered that everyone had a similar answer: The most
important qualification to become a leader is the desire to
get ahead. It was not academic qualifications, not experience
in other jobs, not good looks. **It was desire!**

You had fun coming up with your Personal Mission Statement in the last chapter, you had fun deciding what it is in
life you really want—but as to actually fulfilling that Personal Mission Statement, you may be thinking, "Um,
maybe." Because you have spent so many years refusing to
allow your strong, passionate self to guide your life, it may
be that you think you might have lost your capacity to really
make significant changes.

There's only one way to get over that self-defeating attitude. Set a goal, and go for it! Don't think about all the ram-
ifications of what you're doing, don't worry about the "big
picture," don't worry about the possibility of failure, don't
worry about anything. **Just take some action, no matter how
small it is!** For years at work, I've been seeing what this attitude can accomplish. Many of the women who come to our
company aren't gung-ho salespeople. Many are scared about
taking a first step. Some can't imagine that they will be able
to make a sale, let alone run their own business!

We tell them to simply set a short-term goal for themselves to sell a specific amount of products. That's it. Set a
goal to make a small sale—and see how it feels.

And when they have done it, they cannot believe how
great they feel! **By accomplishing a goal, their feelings about
themselves have changed!**

How to Set Your Own Goals

NOW IT'S YOUR TURN TO WRITE DOWN GOALS—PRECISE ones! The minute you start, you will probably feel a surge of energy. It is amazing how our lives begin to move into a higher gear the moment we aim at something. To quote Henry Ford, who set the kinds of goals for himself that revolutionized the American automobile business, "Thinking always ahead, thinking always of trying to do more, brings a state of mind in which nothing seems impossible."

But beware. Stay alert! That old negative voice inside us can be devious. If it realizes that we really are committed to change, it may try every trick in the book to turn us back to our old ways. And one way it will do it is by trying to make us forget our goals.

The fact is that it's pretty easy for old habits to return because they are so familiar. But there is an easy way to beat that voice. Make a Goal List.

Putting our goals on paper is a symbolic way of saying that this time, we are not fooling around. It is our way of saying that this time, we are going forward.

So do it now, before you turn the page. Write your goals down!

And make sure you write down your goals someplace where they are easily available. It might be on a three-by-five card that you can keep in a pocket. Or it might be on a laminated sheet of paper that stays on the refrigerator. I keep my Goal List in my Day-Timer. No matter how busy I am, I will flip to my Goal List at some point during the day and spend a few minutes reading the goals that are written there. I think about what I am doing that day to accomplish those goals; then I determine what areas I need to focus on for the next day. Most important, just by taking the time to read over my goals, I keep them firmly in sight. I am renewed. My desire to fulfill my dreams remains alive and energized. I even read my Goal List again before I go to sleep at night, in order that ideas can be filtered around in my subconscious.

I know a Goal List seems so simple, but it does work wonders. I have a friend whose Goal List, which she keeps in her purse, consists of the ten things she wants to do before she dies. If she is unsure about a choice that she must make in her daily life, she consults her Goal List. If the choice doesn't appear to have anything to do with her list, then she says no.

Clearly, my friend avoids a lot of indecision in her life. She keeps from spending too much time getting caught up in small, pointless details. Here's a philosophy from which all of us can learn. As we study our own goals, we must determine which ones are absolutely necessary to achieve first. This process might be difficult for those of you who want to do many things—but be patient. If we give ourselves fifty goals, and then head off trying to change everything, we will feel a great sense of frustration. We eventually will feel overwhelmed by everything we have to do.

Remember, we often have to accomplish certain goals first before we are able to accomplish others. For instance, it might be difficult to think about a new career if you haven't gotten your home life in order.

Short-Term and Long-Term Goals

A GOOD BALANCE IS FOR US TO MAINTAIN A MIX OF GOALS for both the immediate future and the distant future. As excited as you might be about achieving great things in life—and I hope you never lose that excitement!—don't forget your smaller, short-term goals. We must set smaller goals for ourselves to help lead us to the big smooth highway in our life, the ideal road. It is a way for us to map out what turns or exits we need to make to reach that dream.

We are often told stories in the media about "overnight successes"—men or women who seemed to have found success all at once. But if you really check out how they made it, you'll discover that they established their own goals and went after them the same way we must go after ours—one step at a time, in which a series of smaller goals were accomplished in order to get to the big one.

Every opportunity, no matter how small, can be a chance to take another step forward. Plus, with smaller goals, it's easier for us to learn to trust ourselves again. This is far more important than you might think. When we tell ourselves that we are going to do something and we don't follow through, we have broken a promise to ourselves—which is even more harmful than breaking a promise to someone else. For years, we have been doing this, teaching our subconscious minds that what we say doesn't really count. Imagine that you say to yourself, "Tomorrow, I'm going to start a workout program," and then you don't do it. What kind of message do you think you're sending to your subconscious? You're telling it not to worry about goals, because you're not going to follow through with them anyway.

We must jolt our subconscious minds back into shape. We need to commit our *whole* mind to following through. And that's why smaller goals work. Let me tell you how I finally learned to set small goals. For more than twenty years, I was the queen of dieters. I was desperate to find a way to get control over my body weight. There were times in my life when I was so anxious to lose ten pounds that it seemed I was unable to think about anything else.

And do you know how I would go about trying to lose

that weight? I'd announce that my goal was to lose ten pounds in the next two weeks. I didn't consider setting reasonable, smaller goals for myself that I could achieve over a period of weeks. I went to the extreme, convincing myself that I could lose that weight simply by not eating much for two weeks! It was ridiculous. I set such an unrealistic goal that I ended up failing!

Of course, I couldn't do it. I'd go for a few days without much food, lose a few pounds, and then go on a horrific eating binge that made me heavier than when I started the diet. But did I think that I should change my goals? No! As the classic deluded dieter, I planned going on an even more severe diet.

One time, I went on a diet in which I ate nothing but hot dogs, bananas, and hard-boiled eggs. I even tried prescription diet pills (those seldom work!—lifestyle change does). And nothing worked—I kept gaining back all my lost weight—until it occurred to me that there had to be a better way to reach my destination. I asked myself, **"Rather than set one extreme goal, why not set a series of smaller goals that can lead me to my bigger goal?"**

So I did just that. Week by week, I gave myself a series of smaller goals in which I slowly cut out a few unhealthy, fattening foods. One week, it would be less sugar (not all sugar). The next week, I would eat less fried food. Meanwhile, I had another series of goals that each week focused on eating smaller portions. Then I committed to exercise! It was actually easy. I didn't deprive myself of anything. No extremes.

And instead of losing ten pounds, I lost seventeen pounds—and kept them off permanently.

The Power of Smaller Goals

*I*T'S ASTONISHING HOW SMALL GOALS CAN WORK MIRACLES. Many people who think they cannot stop smoking finally break their addiction when they set hourly goals. That's right. *Hourly goals.* They resolve not to smoke for one hour, and they resolve to do it again the next hour, and on and on and on. Eventually, they are able to make more ambitious goals for themselves and become smoke-free forever.

Smaller goals are easy to visualize if you think about a long-term goal—like running a marathon. A few years ago, I made the decision to run a twenty-six-mile marathon. From one standpoint, the whole idea of me doing such a thing seemed absurd. At the time, I was only an average jogger. I couldn't run very far before becoming winded. I had no idea whether I was capable of such physical endurance.

But I made it my goal to complete a marathon—and I gave myself one year to prepare for it. I drew up a calendar and mapped out an entire plan, starting at the very beginning in which I mixed walking with jogging. Then I gave myself a goal to be jogging three consecutive miles by a certain date. Then I gave myself another goal to be jogging six miles by a later date, and then, after that, I gave myself a goal to do longer-distance runs on weekends. Next, I had a goal to be running ten miles a day by a certain date. Then my goal was to do a twenty-mile run. Finally, I was ready for a marathon, which I accomplished almost one year after I started training.

By setting a series of smaller goals, I achieved what I had long dreamed about. Regardless of whatever it is we attempt to do, we need to know that we will not be able to do it overnight. We need plans. We need smaller goals to lead to our bigger goals—to our Big Dreams!

A Goal-Setting Exercise

G O BACK NOW AND STUDY THE LIST OF GOALS THAT YOU wrote down earlier in this chapter. Pick one of your biggest, most important long-term goals for your life and write it down in the space below:

Long-Term Goal:

_____!

Now write down five smaller, short-term goals you can set that will help you eventually fulfill the long-term goal. If you can, put in the exact date when you wish to have your smaller goals accomplished.

Short-Term Goals to Reach Long-Term Goal:

1. _____

2. _____

3. _____

4. _____

5. _____

You can use this exercise to help you accomplish any major goal in your life—you are breaking down your major goal into much smaller bites that are much easier to swallow. For those of you whose long-range goal might take a few years or even longer, a series of short-term goals will make your journey onto your new road far more manageable and rewarding.

I would recommend setting deadlines for each of your short-term goals. Just as professors know students won't get their term papers written unless there is a set deadline—and just as corporate executives know that their system will get bogged down unless there are specific production schedules—so we, too, will get to our ultimate destination if we set a series of "target dates" to accomplish our smaller goals.

Visualizing Your Goals

*E*VEN WHEN YOUR GOALS SEEM A LONG WAY OFF, THERE IS one invaluable thing you can do to keep yourself motivated. Visualize yourself having already attained the various goals you have set.

There is no greater aid for you to stay on the right road than visualization. Athletes know it, successful business executives know it, peak performers in every field know it. In order to succeed, you must first see yourself succeeding. In order to become more confident, you must first picture yourself as a person with high self-esteem. If you want a loving relationship in your life, you must first picture yourself as a person worthy of giving and receiving deep romantic love.

Do you remember the old saying I like to use in my talks—that what a person can conceive can be achieved? Or to put it in the words of the great Walt Disney, "If you can dream it, you can do it." By picturing ourselves at our highest levels—imagining ourselves as a finished product, with our goals accomplished—we will become much more focused on our dreams and goals.

Of course, I'm not saying you automatically become what you think about. You must work. But positive visualization will give you an astonishing burst of motivation. By repeatedly imagining yourself accomplishing your goals, you will develop greater confidence and belief in your personal abilities.

Positive visualization is not some abstract concept. It is not a silly, pie-in-the-sky theory. It is a significant factor in determining who succeeds and who fails. No painter, for example, is able to execute a masterpiece without first knowing in his or her mind what the painting will look like. No writer can produce the great American novel without having an idea how that novel will conclude. No architect can construct a magnificent building without first visualizing what that building will be. We, too, must have an inner vision of what our lives will become. And just like the architect, we must have our own blueprint, in which we build our new lives one stone at a time.

Here is what I've often done. I have put a picture in my mind, down to the last detail, of everything I want my life to be. I close my eyes and imagine exactly what my life would look and feel like if my dreams are accomplished. I see my family as a loving close-knit clan. I see myself as a dynamic, caring, and motivated woman, filled with great physical energy and health. I see myself at a desk and in a boardroom, running a company. I see myself receiving genuine respect and accolades for my accomplishments (instead of receiving the false flattery that used to come when people saw me acting out in my "false" role). I see myself enjoying the luxuries that come with financial success. I see myself standing up before a crowd of women and telling them about their own opportunities for success if they simply move their lives in a slightly different direction.

The Reality of Visualization

L ET ME EXPLAIN WHAT'S HAPPENING WHEN YOU AND I VISU-
alize. Scientists who study the brain have learned that
our minds work best through images. In fact, when
you imagine yourself doing something in a certain way, the
mind tends to believe this is a real experience. Stanford University researchers have found that a very strong mental
image can actually turn on the nervous system in the same
way that a "real" image would. Perhaps you have heard the
story of Liu Chi Kung, China's premier concert pianist, who
was imprisoned in 1959 during the political revolution in
China. Liu Chi Kung's arrest was devastating news to the international arts community because only a year earlier, he
had placed second in the international Van Cliburn
Tchaikovsky Competition. He was held for seven years, during which he never touched a piano. When Liu Chi Kung
was released, people assumed he would never regain his
ability. But within a year of his freedom, he gave a concert
tour—and the stunned critics said he was better than he was
before he went to prison.

How did he do it? The musician said that in his jail cell, he
practiced every single day—in his mind! He rehearsed all his
repertoire, over and over, pretending he was at a keyboard.

It is common among professional performers to mentally
rehearse their performances before they go on. The night
before a surgery, Dr. Charles Mayo, for whom the Mayo
Clinic was named, would mentally rehearse everything he
was going to do, from putting on his surgical garb to making his first incision. The members of the U.S. Women's
Gymnastics Team, who won the 1996 Olympic gold medal,
were taught to "visualize" their entire routines prior to
competing.

During a visit several years ago to a medical meeting in Italy, Dr. Charles Garfield, a clinical professor at the UCLA School of Medicine, began listening to some European scientists who had spent millions of dollars on research on how to train athletes for optimum performance. When they began talking about the power of guided imagery, Garfield was skeptical. So they asked him to participate in a research experiment. They took him to a gym, hooked him up to monitors that measured brain waves, heartbeat, and muscle tension, and then asked him to attempt to bench-press as much as he could.

Under enormous strain, Dr. Garfield raised 300 pounds of weight. He said he might be able, if he was lucky, to lift ten pounds more—but that was it.

The scientists, however, asked Garfield to relax, breathe deeply, and imagine lifting not just ten pounds more, but twenty pounds more. For more than thirty minutes, they had him visualize grabbing the bar, and successfully pushing it up. After several mental rehearsals, they put him back down on the bench and asked him to lift the barbell above him. Garfield lifted it easily.

It wasn't just 310 pounds. It was 365 pounds! And the scientists were certain they could get him up to 400 pounds. All this from a man who was not in top physical condition!

Now do you understand why visualization is one of the most powerful tools you have to keep you on the right road? Garfield became so convinced about the power of visualization that he began to research the topic himself when he returned to the United States. He found that most high achievers in American business do some sort of visualization without necessarily knowing what it's called. "They see in their mind's eye the result they want, and the actions leading to it," Garfield wrote. "They visualize, not as a substitute for thorough preparation and hard work, but as an indispensable adjunct."

As we learned early on in this book, how we talk to ourselves—the beliefs that we hold about who we are and what we are capable of doing—not only shapes our self-image, it also determines our reality. The quality of our lives is based upon the mental pictures that we allow to run through our brains like one long, continuous movie.

Some of you reading this may still think the whole idea of positive visualization may not work. Let me remind you that most of us already have spent much of our lives practicing *negative visualization*. We are experts at creating future scenes in our minds in which we feel unsuccessful. We have created very detailed scenes in which we make an embarrassing mistake, or fall flat on our face in front of others. For years, we've been allowing our negative visualization to hold us back emotionally and to keep us from taking any chances at success and discovering what a fulfilled life is all about.

If negative visualization can have such an impact on our lives, think what *positive visualization* will do! Instead of starting off the day expecting strain and tension, what if we started off the day expecting to feel joy about the challenges that lay ahead? Instead of expecting we will be exhausted by the end of that day, what if we imagined ourselves energized and refreshed?

One psychologist has said that what we hold in our mind is what we move toward. It's true. We will stay on our new road, moving toward our dreams—as long as we hold the most positive images in our mind. At this point, we are limited only by the self-portrait we hold in our mind. If the movie is one filled with the most positive images—showing what we really want and what we really can achieve—then it's guaranteed that the reality of our lives will change, too.

A Visualization Exercise for You

NOW IT'S TIME TO TRY IT. IT'S TIME FOR YOU TO VISUAL-ize how you want your future to look. You're going to picture a scene in your future *as if it is happening right now!* You're going to try to involve all the senses in imagining this scene: you not only want to see this future experience, but you want to hear the sounds, feel and even smell the sensations of this experience.

The important thing to remember is to be specific—to make sure you walk through every single part of the scene you are about to visualize. This kind of visualization is like a guided fantasy—and you are in control of determining how the fantasy turns out. You get to decide how you want it to be. You get to determine exactly what will happen from moment to moment. You get to be a complete success—and you get to do it without having to deal with any negative image whatsoever!

Get in the most comfortable position you know. It could be sitting down, or lying in your bed, or sprawled on your favorite couch. You might want to play your favorite, most soothing music. You might want to turn down the lights. Do whatever makes you feel most at peace and relaxed.

Next, take a deep breath (the kind you can feel at the bottom of your lungs). Inhale through your nose slowly so that you feel the tension in your body beginning to drain away. Exhale slowly and then inhale again, this time holding the air in your lungs for several seconds. Keep thinking about relaxing.

Again, breathe in deeply and out—very slowly.

Feel . . . yourself . . . relaxing.

Each time, as you hold your breath, give yourself a silent affirmation: "I am worthy of success." "I am worthy of love." "I am worthy of happiness." "I am worthy of great confidence."

At this point, visualize one of many things. You might want to picture a scene of your marriage functioning at its best. Or perhaps an ideal evening with your family. You could picture yourself as a great financial success. For the purposes of this exercise, however, let's have you visualize yourself making a major presentation at a meeting in which you must persuade a group of people to accept your project or product.

Imagine yourself getting dressed for the meeting. Envision what you would wear. Think about smiling serenely into your mirror as you apply your makeup. Take yourself out the front door and into your car and toward the office. Picture yourself with light all around you.

Now see yourself arriving at an office building, striding confidently through the door. Notice the way people greet you, how intrigued they are by you, and how they give you a second look as they walk away. Imagine yourself opening the door to a conference room and saying good morning in an enthusiastic voice to the group that has been assembled to hear your presentation. Look everyone straight in the eye. Take note of the way your audience seems to be leaning forward in anticipation. They are fascinated by you. You can feel it. There is an energy in this room—and it's being caused by you.

And now you begin to speak. Your voice is firm, not overly dramatic, but filled with the kind of persuasive power that your audience rarely hears. As you talk, you can see smiles playing at the edges of people's lips. It's as if they cannot get enough of you! During the question-and-answer period, more ideas surface, and you discuss them articulately, your body language strong, confident, relaxed.

When you are finished, they burst into applause. You do not even need to hear the clapping, for you already know your presentation is a success!

Incorporate Visualization into Your Daily Life

AS YOU START YOUR NEW JOURNEY, IT IS A GOOD IDEA TO spend at least ten minutes a day doing these kinds of visualization exercises. You can do them anywhere— fixing dinner, grocery shopping, taking a bath. Your list of potential visualizations is endless. You could create a scene, for example, in which you step on the scales and weigh exactly what you desire. If you do that particular visualization ten days in a row, you will find yourself eating more healthfully and getting the right amount of exercise. Why? Because if you imagine yourself doing something in a particular way often enough, you will tend to do that thing in the way you imagine it. With enough visualization, your *positive images* will overtake your *negative images*, and you will have no doubt about your ability to stay on your particular road and make great changes for the future.

You might also want to try a different kind of visualization called picture imaging. Do you remember when we were kids and we cut out magazine photographs or bought posters of our heroes and heroines? Although we didn't know it, what we were doing was visualizing a future for ourselves. We were giving ourselves an image of what we would like to be.

Who says we can't do the same thing as adults? Remember the friend of mine who was capable at almost everything except public speaking? She once saw a magazine photo of a well-known female business leader giving a speech to a large crowd. My friend cut it out and put it on the bulletin board in her office. Every time she got up from behind her desk, she saw it and thought about it. Did the picture itself turn her into a great public speaker? Of course not. But the picture did make her more and more comfortable with the idea that she could do the same thing herself.

Putting up a picture where we can see it helps bring to the surface our subconscious desires. Some people make what is called a Futures Collage. They cut out several pictures from old magazines of things that represent the kind of future they want. They then paste all the pictures to a poster board. There could be a picture of a family having dinner in a beautiful dining room, one of a woman in a Chanel suit striding down Fifth Avenue in New York, and another of a glorious vacation spot.

I recommend your Futures Collage be photos of real people—not just of models playacting. Seeing real people doing the things you dream about can be a great inspiration for you. Think what could happen if you put your Futures Collage on your refrigerator and stared at it every morning. You would realize that you, too, are a person just like the people in the photographs.

Finally, some people create a Dream Book. They choose five or ten things they dream most about having in life, find a photograph for each dream, and then put each photograph on a different page of a notebook. In the mornings or evenings, they leaf through their Dream Book, seeing their dreams.

If you have difficulty with visualizing, write the following down on a piece of paper and hold it in your hands as you relax in your favorite chair.

Describe yourself, what you're wearing, how you smell, what the weather is like. Write down a positive, confident feeling; see yourself in every detail. Now you will have a written guide to help you get started.

These small, simple techniques can work wonders! By visualizing yourself, over and over, thinking the right thoughts and doing the right things, you are doing nothing less than reprogramming your mind. You are imprinting upon your subconscious the fact that you are someone who is going to achieve whatever it is you set out to achieve. I guarantee you, absolutely nothing will be able to stop you from your journey.

Staying the Course

How to Stay on the Right Road Now That You've Found It

We might still sometimes hear the last desperate gasps of our old voice trying to draw us back into our old negative life. We might still hear the voice of fear that has guided us for so long down so many roads. But now we know something new. We never again have to follow those voices!

Driving Lessons

How to Avoid Curbs, Bad Drivers, and Flat Tires

Consider a mistake you make in life as nothing more than a flat tire. As long as you're prepared for it, it won't be all that overwhelming when it happens. Flat tires (mistakes!) do not have to signal an end to your journey. In truth, they can signal that you're going to have a much better journey. If you change tires, you're guaranteed to have a smoother ride.

AND NOW, SUDDENLY, WE'RE HERE.

We have learned to clean our interiors, overhaul our engines, balance our tires, and take control of the steering wheel. We have discovered that we do not have to be prisoners of our past, we do not have to depend on false roles that hold us back, and we do not have to drift aimlessly through our days.

We are taking control of our destinies. **We're on the right road!** We are determining our future! We are on our way to tasting the fruits of our own hopes and dreams!

And even as I say this, I expect there are some who are thinking, "Come on, Jinger, that's all there is to it? Aren't there huge hurdles that I still must surmount? Won't there be a great crisis or two to overcome? Don't I have to go through years of further struggle before I know for sure that I'm a different person?"

Before you ask another question, hit the "pause" button in your brain.

What I want you to understand is that the voice you hear asking all these questions is not your real voice—not at all! It's the last desperate gasps of your old negative voice trying to draw you back into your old life. You're hearing the voice of fear that has guided you for so long down too many un-happy roads. **And do you realize that even though you might still hear that voice, you don't have to listen to it?**

Do you remember, early in the book, when we talked about our long-neglected inner voice? The quiet voice that has been begging us for years to clean our inner engines of self-doubt and anxiety? The voice that has been telling us that we don't have to live the same way? The voice telling us that we have been put on this earth to succeed?

Well, over the last several chapters, you have been learning to listen to that inner voice in a way you never have before. You have been cutting out not only destructive messages, but also those messages that have distracted you from your most noble purposes in life. You have become aware of one of your out-of-date attitudes. In various small ways, you have rediscovered "you-at-your-best"!

Already, you have begun following the special part of you that is unlike anyone else. Just you! The one who sees the world in a way that is all your own! You have tapped into those "extra" qualities in you that can turn the ordinary into the extraordinary!

So congratulate yourself. This is a time of great jubilation.

But remain on guard. Just because we are now on the right road, it would be naïve for us to expect that there will be no bumps. Change—especially when it comes to one's inner life—always comes in small increments. Indeed, our "old" self-image that has prevailed for the greater part of our lives is not going to be killed off with one great pronouncement that we have "changed." We have to stay diligent about keeping our car on the road.

Now let's go through a few driving lessons to make sure that happens.

Lesson 1. Try Not to Slam the Pedal to the Metal

ALL THROUGH THIS BOOK I'VE BEEN TELLING YOU ABOUT THE joys of finding a new road and viewing an unlimited horizon—and now that you're there, I'm asking you to drive the speed limit, to take your time and smell the roses.

Actually, entering this phase of your life is just like learning to drive a car. If you go too slowly, you'll either stall out or you'll be so intimidated by the faster traffic racing past you that you'll end up on the side of the road. And if you go too fast, you'll quickly lose control, hitting curbs or ending up in a ditch or wrecking your car.

One ancient philosopher noted, "A journey of a thousand miles must begin with a single step."

That's all. A single step. Great acts of change don't come quickly. They don't come because you're going faster than everyone else. "Great acts are performed not through strength but by perseverance," Samuel Johnson once wrote. No truer words could be spoken. Our journey is built on perseverance—not speed.

So as you enter this new realm of your life, be gentle pushing down on the accelerator. If you rush through the process, you'll get exhausted, and you may eventually decide to switch back to your old way of life—your old roads. As soon as you learn you don't have to drive as fast as you can in order to make your new life fulfilling, the less stressful your journey will be.

Lesson 2. Be Prepared for Bad Drivers

IF YOU'RE NOT WATCHING OUT FOR BAD DRIVERS, THEY WILL run you off the road. Some of them will even do it intentionally, some of them unintentionally. But the result will be the same. Your journey will come to a sudden halt.

In your own journey to personal success, you are going to find people—some of whom will be your friends—who, even unconsciously, resent what you're doing and would prefer that you go back to your old way of life. These are people who haven't found the courage to change their own lives, and they feel secure only if everyone stays on the same road they do.

These are the people who will come to you, seemingly with all the best intentions in the world, and say, "Are you *sure* you want to start a new career?" "Are you *convinced* that going back to school and leaving your family a few hours a day is the right thing for you?" "Aren't you *scared?*" They are sending you negative messages, suggesting that you abandon your ideals and be like everyone else. They are trying to run you off your road.

You will have conflicts with some old friends. The nature of your friendship might eventually change: they prefer the old system in which you call each other to complain about life—and you want a new system in which you call each other to celebrate your new beginnings. As you get started on this journey, it might behoove you to have a few long talks with the people closest to you—including your husband, if you're married—to make sure they support you. You might want to have a talk with your parents and siblings. Let's say you grew up in a family of lawyers and you decide you're going to go a different way and become a fashion designer. There is nothing wrong whatsoever in your choice of careers—nothing at all. But I expect you're going to have to deal with some raised eyebrows from family members who may have very little respect for fashion as a career. And instead of letting you drive the way you want, they might try nudging you off your road and getting you back onto their road. Even if they have the best intentions, they're still being poor drivers.

Lesson 3. Make Sure You're Around Good Drivers

INSTEAD OF BEING AFFECTED BY THOSE UNHAPPY FOLKS WHO want company, look for people who are driving in your direction. Let's face it—they are people who are winners like you. They love success, and they love celebrating your success. It's amazing how the most successful people are thrilled with others who become successful. The unsuccessful—the people going in the other direction—want to see you lose the way they have.

As you begin your journey, there's nothing more reassuring than having some cars around that are going along with you. You'll feel more courageous. You can look out your window and see people like yourself, determined to do something significant with their lives. These are people who care about how you're doing and who will encourage you to keep trying during times of stress. You'll realize it's much easier to stay on your new road if you don't always try to "go it alone." Keep supporters around you as much as you can. That way, you'll never feel lonely on your new road—and you'll make sure to have protection from the other drivers who are stalling along the road.

As you travel on your journey, you'll find it amazingly helpful to get to know some of the superstar drivers you'll meet along the way. These are people who can be your role models. They might be leaders in the particular business you have chosen for yourself, or they could be philosophers or authors or entrepreneurs or motivators. You might never become their best friend, but don't let that stop you. You'll be surprised at how enriched and enlivened you'll feel simply by shaking their hands if you come across them at an airport or at an event. These are people who started where you did, who established goals and values for themselves, then beat back their fears and accomplished what they set out to do. These kinds of winners have an aura about them that will stimulate your own drive and excitement to keep heading down your new road.

I not only love to meet successful people I admire, but I realize I have developed mentors for various parts of my life. For example, I talk with women who have been entrepreneurial successes and I take walks in the mornings with a wise, articulate woman whom I view as my mentor for personal issues. To me, these different women are teachers, coaches, and motivators. They tell me when they think I'm in the wrong gear, and they guide me by sharing their beliefs.

Obviously, I'm not suggesting that you lose yourself by trying to perfectly imitate the superstar drivers. Do learn to celebrate your own uniqueness. But you can learn so much by watching the behavior of superstars.

Lesson 4. Be Prepared for Flat Tires

DO YOU REMEMBER THE FIRST TIME YOU HAD TO DEAL WITH A flat tire? You either stood helplessly on the side of the road, hoping a Good Samaritan would come to your assistance, or got down on your hands and knees to take the flat tire off yourself and replace it with a spare. No doubt you thought the whole process would never end. It was dirty, uncomfortable, and you may have been nervous that you didn't tighten the bolts enough to keep the new tire attached to the wheel! Finally, you got back on the road, fearing your car might never drive the same way again.

For experienced drivers, flat tires are just a normal part of the journey. They know that no car, regardless of how good it is, can go forever without one of its tires losing air. As a result, they have become capable of changing their tires and getting back on the road in no time. They don't let a flat tire upset them: they know it doesn't mean their car is broken. They fix their tire, and they move on.

Consider a mistake you make in life as nothing more than a flat tire. As long as you're prepared for it, it won't be all that overwhelming when it happens. Flat tires (mistakes!) do not have to signal an end to your journey. In truth, they can signal that you're going to have a much better journey. If you change tires, you're guaranteed to have a smoother ride. And if you learn from a mistake, you're guaranteed to figure out how to be that much more successful in the future.

At work, we have a policy of never seeing our mistakes or errors as "failures." We refuse to be disappointed when we experience any setback at our company. Ironically, my husband, Dick, and I have learned that true success is made up just as much from failure as it is from success. The more times we have "failed," the faster we have learned to get back on our road to success and go forward. No longer do we see problems as "barriers" but as opportunities to improve. We recognize our mistakes (or flats) and use them as a step to improvement.

I like to say that we have "stubborn sight." By that I mean we stubbornly refuse to see ourselves as failures. If a project fails, we are not failures. We see only the best of all possible worlds. Every problem gives us a special chance to prosper. Every mistake becomes a valuable tool to make a better product or service. Every setback is nothing more than an opportunity to learn something more about ourselves, and our company.

I doubt that there is a successful business executive in this country who has not been on the brink of failure. Pick the most successful people you know, and if you study their biographies, you will discover that they encountered deep trouble before building their own fortunes. They could have surrendered and said, "There's no way I can win." Instead, they studied their mistakes and learned what to do the next time. The more they studied their setbacks, the more they realized they were not facing impossible odds. They simply had a flat tire that needed fixing.

A lot of people who start their journey make the mistake of defining success as being "perfect." I don't even define success as "doing your best every moment of the day." There are times during a typical day when you're not going to be at your best. After all, you're only human. Reading more of this book—or reading a hundred more like it—won't make you a superwoman. That's why I try to follow what I call the "80–20" rule. At the end of the day, I'll look back on what's happened and ask myself, "Did I get through eighty percent of this day doing my best?" Note that I didn't ask myself, "Did I get through eighty percent of this day accomplishing everything I wanted to accomplish?" I didn't ask, "Did I get through eighty percent of the day coming out on top in all my ventures?" I simply ask if 80 percent of what I did that day was done with sincerity, commitment, positive actions, and an eye on my goals. If so, then I've been successful, and I know that's enough to make whatever I'm setting out to do happen.

Remember, if you aren't getting flat tires, then you're not moving forward. Flat tires are signs of success. Fix them, and you'll enjoy your journey more than you ever have before!

Lesson 5. Honk Your Horn!

I REALLY BELIEVE IT'S IMPORTANT TO OCCASIONALLY HONK YOUR horn just for the joy of it. Or to put it another way: Show your enthusiasm for the journey you've undertaken! Celebrate the magnificence of your adventure!

Of the many secrets to success, the one that is often most underrated is "enthusiasm." To be sure, when Dick and I started our company, we knew we had to be thoroughly educated about the business of cosmetics and sales. We needed a mission statement, a clear set of goals, and absolute deadlines to meet those goals. We had to be committed, and at times we put in very long hours. But, like anyone else starting a new business, we found ourselves staying up late at night completing tasks that we didn't expect we'd have to do. I was literally sweeping floors, cleaning bathrooms, and painting the company's machinery. It would have been easy for Dick and me to turn to each other and say, "Look, this isn't what we thought it was going to be. Let's bail out." **But at that very moment, we made sure to express greater enthusiasm!** We talked as if we were already on top of the world even though, at that time, we most definitely were not!

Why did we do such a thing? Enthusiasm is the best antidote you have for mental fatigue. Acting enthusiastic about your particular project keeps you motivated and focused. Your mind doesn't wander: you aren't spending excess energy worrying about little things or thinking about some past event that's no longer important. Try it sometime. When you feel yourself slowing down or getting discouraged about the work you're doing, take a break and tell yourself how excited you are that you have the opportunity to do what you are doing.

When I used to be on my hands and knees, painting our old machinery, I would find myself saying, "This contraption is starting to look beautiful! It's really beautiful!" Does that sound silly? Of course it does. But the simple expression of enthusiasm gave me a sense of pride about what I was doing. It reminded me that accomplishing this little task was important to help lead us to the more significant tasks.

It's true, as psychologists have often said, that feelings follow actions: the more you *act* a certain way, the more you *feel* that way. Accordingly, by acting excited about what you're doing, especially on those gloomy days that are filled with thankless tasks, your self-esteem does not falter. It's truly amazing what happens to your personality as long as you make a determined effort to remain positive. What will determine the course of your life more than any other one thing is whether or not you're willing to show optimism even in times when you feel complete discomfort.

Enthusiastic people don't wait for their "ship to come in." They don't believe in waiting, period. They deal with problems as soon as they come up. They don't spend time worrying, because worrying doesn't help lessen the problem. They use their zest and drive to find solutions.

So honk your horn! Keep acting as if you are already successful, and you inevitably will be!

Lesson 6. Never Take Your Eyes Off the Road

AS SIMPLISTIC A PIECE OF ADVICE AS THIS IS, IT IS THE MISTAKE we tend to make more than any other. We literally do it when we drive a car, and we do it just as often when we set off in a new personal direction. We start looking at the signs and the scenery and bang!—we're hitting curbs and we're landing in the same old ruts.

There is a price we must pay for our entry onto a new road in life, and that is that we must always keep looking forward. If we do not stay focused on what lies ahead, we will start listening again to our old voice and we will drift away, back into the wilderness.

You may have come up with the finest Personal Mission Statement ever written and you may have the perfect list of clearly defined goals. You may know exactly what short-term goals you need to accomplish in order to reach your long-term goals. You may know exactly what you want to do with your life five years from now, ten years from now, and twenty years from now.

But please hear this! **None of your planning will do any good if you are not vigilant about where you are going.** The truth is that all the self-understanding that may have come since you started reading this book can disappear if you take your eyes off where you're going. As idealistic as you are about changing your life, no change will come to you by chance. You must take some action every day to make sure you are keeping your eyes on the road.

I used to wake up in the morning full of great plans about change—yet as the day progressed, I would lose my self-discipline to follow through. I'd wake up the next day and do the same thing all over again. And as each day would pass, I became more tempted to get down on myself and give up.

You might go through the same problem as your journey begins. Once again, please remember: Go slowly (just go!). **This program of self-change that you have been learning is not designed to make you perfect. It's designed to get you moving forward—and to help keep you moving forward.**

The Path of Change

S OME DAYS, YOU'LL FEEL YOU HAVE IMPROVED THE RICH-ness of your life by almost 100 percent. Some days, it will be only a few percent.

But that's okay—because you're changing! You've taken that courageous leap forward. You have opened the door and you are stepping out, leaving behind an old identity. You are driving adventurously into the unknown. It's the experience of moving toward the goal that's important!

Some are going to change at a faster pace than others. What works for one might not work for someone else.

Some might be embarking on major career changes, others on building the right relationship. Naturally, those roads are going to be somewhat different. In fact, everybody's road is unique—which is why it is so important to find joy in the journey as it takes place. Instead of being anxious about the destination—instead of worrying about who's doing better than you—the better attitude would be to celebrate the fact that you are traveling forward, too! As has been said before, the game of life is not about the final score but about the playing. You might not discover the cure for cancer, or you might not run a multimillion-dollar corporation. But if you live life to its fullest, whatever that kind of life is, then you have become a winner. If you drive down your road with bravery and courtesy, with intensity and goodwill, with honesty and enthusiasm, victories will inevitably come your way.

There is a saying: "Today is the first day of the rest of your life." Every day, you have the opportunity when you wake up to be "Positively You." No matter how many setbacks you experience, the next day you have the very same opportunity to do your best, every minute of the day, which is all we need ask of ourselves. This is one of the most reassuring feelings I know—to recognize that every day I have a new chance to connect to the most powerful part of myself, no matter the results of the day before.

Balancing Your Wheels

How to Keep Harmony in Your Life Even as You Change

Although it seems as if the world is divided between two groups of people—one group that says, "Don't just sit there, do something," and the other group that says, "Don't just do something, sit there"—the truth is that with a little discipline and some smart planning, we can live in both worlds.

ONE OF THE THINGS THAT MY FATHER TAUGHT ME IN CHILDHOOD was that if the four wheels of a car weren't properly aligned and balanced, then we were in for a bumpy ride. Without balanced wheels, our cars pull to one side or the other, and soon we'll find ourselves losing control.

Balance! Of all the books that give us advice about how to succeed, we are rarely told about how we can be successful while maintaining a balanced life. For me, a person cannot be successful unless he or she has balance. A successful life is not outhustling others. It is not working longer hours. It is not being richer than your neighbors. As I said in the Introduction, to ensure a smoother, happier ride through life, we must make an effort to balance the important parts of our lives—to balance our wheels!

Indeed, if just one of our wheels is weak, the entire car is weak. If we deflate the wheel that powers our families, for example, or if we deflate the wheel that powers our own mental and spiritual needs, then we're in danger of having a wreck and causing serious damage to our lives.

As much as I have a burning desire to accomplish many things in my life and to reach certain goals in my career, I know that the true definition of success is balance. Balance enriches my life, it brings me harmony and peace, and it enriches my perspective on what it means to be truly alive. I am much happier when I am able to balance the needs of my work with the needs of myself and my family—when I can balance my attitudes about structure with attitudes about spontaneity. Balance reminds me that I work to live, not live to work. It keeps me from being consumed by my daily "to do" list. It allows me, even in the midst of my very public occupation, to give myself private time. And it has me stop and cherish simple pleasures even on the most hectic of days.

All four wheels on our car need focus—they are the four main areas of our lives. Those are our **Work Wheel, Home Wheel, People Wheel,** and **Self Wheel.** Our Work Wheel, of course, encompasses our job or career. Our Home Wheel covers our relationship with our family. Our People Wheel encompasses our relationship with our friends and coworkers, and our Self Wheel our relationship with ourselves (spiritual and emotional).

It's one thing to set terrific goals in order to get our Work Wheel rolling forward, but if we don't have goals for the other wheels in our life, we won't find ourselves moving successfully down the road. Our lives will be misaligned. We will not feel complete, or, worse, we will feel stressed, over-whelmed, and pulled in too many directions.

How Imbalanced Is Your Life?

ARE YOU ONE OF THOSE WHO BELIEVE YOUR LIFE IS OUT OF balance? More than ever, women now feel forced to "do it all," and we feel more and more out of con-trol. Our time, space, and energy seem absorbed by tasks or by the needs of others. We make surprisingly irrational de-mands on ourselves. We do not know how or where to draw boundary lines to protect ourselves. We don't feel we are spending enough time with our families, our friends, or by ourselves—and then we feel we don't remain focused enough in our jobs and careers.

Here is a good exercise to see just how balanced your life is. On a calendar or a Day-Timer, keep a detailed schedule of what you do in an average week. And I mean *detailed!* Write down when you get up, and then keep a log of everything you do throughout the day. Make your daily calendar as spe-cific as those of business lawyers who keep track of what they work on every minute of their day so they know how much to bill their clients. If you read a magazine for fifteen minutes while eating lunch, put that down. If you talk to a friend for twenty minutes on a Monday while taking a walk with her, put that down. That's very important!

Then, using four different colored pencils, color-code

your schedule. Each color represents a different wheel. Let's say green will be your Work Wheel, blue will be your Home Wheel, yellow will be your People Wheel, and red your Self Wheel.

Just by looking at the amount of colors in a typical week, you'll discover where your life is out of balance. You'll see where you have spent hours focusing for too long in one area when you could have used that time being more constructive in another area. You'll also realize that sometimes, when you think you're doing one thing, you're really doing something else. How many times, for example, when you are talking to a friend, are you really thinking about all the things you need to do when you get off the phone? How many times during a meeting at work does your mind list the errands you need to do? Or how many times, when you are at home having dinner with your family, do you start thinking about work?

What is happening is that you are not setting clear boundaries for each significant wheel in your life. Your wheels are spinning, blurring one another. You are often not "present" with your friends or your children, even when you are with them, because your mind is cluttered with everything else going on in your life. This is when we have to *stop* spinning and clearly *be* where we are at the time.

Kicking Your Tires

W HAT'S CLEAR TO A LOT OF PEOPLE WHO GO THROUGH a color-coding exercise is that a large reason for unbalanced lives is a lack of prior planning. I know this all too well. I had to learn that the best way for me to get some balance was to schedule it.

That's right. **I learned to schedule balance.**

At the start of every week, I'd write down everything I wanted to do that week for the four different wheels of my life. Then, on my calendar, I would try to find places to focus purely on those wheels. I'd "color in" a couple of hours on a certain afternoon each week, for example, to be with my daughter. In those two hours, I let myself do nothing more than focus on her and let her guide what we did. Did it cut into my work time? Of course it did. But, in turn, I would find another place on my calendar to get in those two extra hours of work.

What I was doing was the equivalent of walking around my car and kicking my tires, making sure they were full of air. It was also my way of checking on the alignment of my car to keep the wheels balanced. Now, I put down everything I do on my calendar. I set aside special times in the morning to work out (part of my Self Wheel), and certain afternoons and evenings to spend time only with my family (Home Wheel). I schedule my time at the office, where I know my secretary won't put through any personal calls (Work Wheel), as well as dinners with our closest friends (People Wheel).

Does this mean I have always spent equal amounts of time in every important area of my life? Of course not. There were plenty of times when I became consumed by a single project. For example, I would occasionally have to go through a "crunch period" at work, one that would bury me in work for two weeks or so. I would have to put off other things—my friends, my self time, and even times with my own daughter. But, early on, I made it clear to her that after the crunch was over, I would have a large block of time carved out in my calendar for the two of us to do things together—whether it was to take a trip or just hang out. Because my daughter knew there would be plenty of time for the two of us to be together at a very specific period in the future, she felt far safer and more secure and not as upset as she might have been during those two weeks when I was buried in work.

Setting Goals for Your Wheels

AFTER DOING ALL THE EXERCISES FROM CHAPTER 9, YOU might know a lot more about setting goals. Let's make sure that these goals help lead us toward a balanced life. Do you have similar goals to build intimacy between you and your children? Do you have goals to set aside time for yourself each day in order to think or improve your own inner spiritual life? These goals, of course, are just as important as the goals we have to become financially successful. What's sad is that too few of us specifically set spiritual goals.

Instead of overloading with goals in one category, I have found our lives can be much more satisfying—and certainly more balanced—if we set different goals for each of our wheels.

Here's how to do it. Instead of making just another random list (earn a six-figure salary, spend the summer in Europe, and so on), visualize your goals in terms of your four wheels. As you set goals for these wheels, here are some sample questions you might want to ask yourself.

Home Wheel If our home is where the most emotional moments of our lives happen, what kind of goals can I set to improve my home life? If I have a family, do I want to set a goal for myself to carve out more time in my schedule to focus on my children? Would a good goal for my life be to set up a weekly "date" with my husband so we could be sure to have more intimate time together? Or, if I'm living alone, are there ways to create a more soothing home environment to provide more comfort? If I'm not married and want to be, do I set goals that will allow me to meet and develop a relationship with the right kind of man?

Here are my personal goals for my Home Wheel.

1. Set mother/daughter afternoon date.

2. Visit with Dick before every evening meal we have together.

3. Refuse to talk business at home.

4. Continue to create systems to simplify my home life.

5. Watch less TV and play board games with Dick and Brittany, my daughter.

Now you do it.

Goals for Your Home Wheel

1. _____

2. _____

3. _____

4. _____

5. _____

People Wheel Knowing that good friendships are vital to emotional health, what goals can I set to develop friends or to improve the friendships that I have? Would it be a beneficial goal to find someone new and interesting to take to lunch one day a month? Would it be beneficial to clear my schedule for an hour a week and call an old friend just to catch up with her? And, similarly, if there is a high-maintenance type of person or coworker who is taking up too much time in my life, would it be wise to set up more definite boundaries with that person? If I feel lonely, what goals could I set to get involved in more social groups? Do I want to set a goal for myself to find a worthwhile community organization that I could join and help champion? Are there goals I can set in order to communicate more pleasantly with others, or to articulate my feelings in a clearer way, or to express myself with more enthusiasm?

Here are my personal goals for my People Wheel.

1. I will communicate with people from the "I" position. I will communicate what I hear, see, feel, and experience.

2. I will no longer spend my precious time with consistently negative people.

3. Real friends know and understand my heart. Therefore, I will no longer feel guilty when I can't be everywhere I'm invited to be.

4. When I am with a person I choose to be with, I will be present and really enjoy listening to that person.

5. I will strive to be emotionally healthy when communicating with people.

Now you do it.

Goals for Your People Wheel

1. _____

2. _____

3. _____

4. _____

5. _____

Work Wheel While most people want more prestige and a larger income in their careers, what are specific goals that will help you get there? Are there particular goals you could set that, if accomplished, will guarantee you more income? Ask yourself: Are there goals I could set that would help me command more authority and responsibility at my job? Or do I want to set goals to enter a new profession altogether? If I am a homemaker and my work involves raising children, what are some goals I can set to create emotionally healthy, intelligent, happy children? If I want to make some money while staying at home, can I set a goal for myself to find part-time work?

Here are my Work Wheel goals.

1. I will think before I speak.

2. If there is a personality conflict with a coworker, I will be aware that we have difficulty and try to hear that person's position as she/he sees it.

3. I will remind myself daily that my career is not just about me. The good of the company is greater than just my personal desires.

4. I will remember my customer above all.

5. I will strive to enjoy my work and know that challenges help me grow and give me problem-solving skills.

Now you do it.

Goals for Your Work Wheel

1. _____

2. _____

3. _____

4. _____

5. _____

Self Wheel Considering that all too often I get caught up in the dailiness of life, what goals can I set just to take care of myself? Do I need to set goals to become more physically fit? What goals would improve my spiritual life? How about setting a goal to clear my mind and pray or meditate fifteen minutes a day as a way to stay in touch with my inner voice? How about writing about my feelings every day in my journal? Are there goals I can set to make sure I can enjoy the little pleasures in life? How about a goal to set aside time every Saturday afternoon for a hobby that I love—like sewing or gardening or reading?

Here are my personal goals for my Self Wheel.

1. I will pray and meditate daily.

2. I will exercise daily, not just for my body, but for my sanity.

3. I will accept whatever life brings to me today, knowing that I can choose how I respond to difficulty.

4. I will stop comparing myself to others, as it injures my spirit. I will remind myself that God created me.

5. I will set time for "fun" and schedule it each week.

Now you do it.

Goals for Your Self Wheel

1. _____

2. _____

3. _____

4. _____

5. _____

Is it really possible to find a balanced life? To get up each morning, determined to get things accomplished—and also to fit in some time to "go with the flow"? To be career-minded—and to take the time to watch a sunset? I guarantee you, it is possible!

Although it seems as if the world is divided between two groups of people—one group that says, "Don't just sit there, do something," and the other group that says, "Don't just do something, sit there"—the truth is that with a little discipline and some smart planning, we can live in both worlds. We can have balance. In many ways, I feel as if this is the most important thing that I can pass on. Through balance, we can learn to live in the moment. And when that happens, we can go down any road that we want in life. Reminder: This single moment will _never_ come again!

Final Tip: Rest Stops!

SOMETIMES, TO IMPROVE THE QUALITY OF LIFE, YOU HAVE TO figure out ways to decrease the quantity of things you do. The problem is that when you launch off on a great new journey, as you are doing now, you sometimes forget to take a break.

As you might have guessed, "rest stops" are those times in your journey when you need to pull over, relax, and fill up with gasoline so that you are replenished with energy. Without rest stops, your mind, body, and spirit will slowly deteriorate. Your mind will become fatigued and empty. There's no way around it. As excited as you might be about your new journey, if you do not take rest stops, you will burn out so quickly you won't know what hit you.

I'm not talking about an annual vacation. I'm talking about a daily rest stop of ten or fifteen minutes in which you clear your mind of all our world's anxiety. Most great people in history have regularly stopped what they were doing and simply shut down for a while. They've retreated in order to replenish themselves. I know it sounds contradictory that you must periodically "stop" in order to successfully go forward. But rest stops give you the chance to reconnect to your imagination, your famous female intuition, and your creativity. And what's amazing is that it doesn't require any kind of serious "thinking." **You simply have to relax!**

Have you ever wondered, for instance, why you get a brilliant flash of insight when you are not thinking? You might be walking in the park and the answer to a problem suddenly comes to you. Or you could be daydreaming about one thing and an idea explodes in your brain about another. By taking a "rest stop," you are allowing yourself to tap into your beautiful unconscious, to unleash the genius inside you. All you have to do is let your mind drift!

For a lot of us, this is harder than it sounds. We're used to going full speed ahead, to working until we are exhausted, and then getting up the next day and starting all over. It's as if we're on autopilot! Many of us are not capable of enjoying a true rest stop because we feel as if we "should" be doing something productive.

Yet there is nothing more productive than taking "time out" to decompress from our often hectic lives. When we do, we can return to our lives filled with a new creativity and excitement!

There are two ways to take a rest stop—both of which are important. First, part of your rest stop should involve "solitude"—being alone. Solitude is vital because it allows you to hear the stirring of your deepest thoughts. It allows you to hear your female intuition. It lets you refocus your attention on what matters most—your soul. Beware: It is so easy in this world to become inundated by other people's attitudes and comments. You can become so "peopled out" that you will lose your own mental clarity without realizing it. You will have trouble again hearing that "inner voice" that we talked about several chapters ago—the voice that can lead you to fulfill your greatest potential.

Solitude, incidentally, is not sitting alone in a room with the television on. It's sitting alone in the room in silence. Deep meditation works great for many people, but I do not believe you have to practice "meditating" in order to obtain the benefits of solitude. If it works for you to repeat a mantra over and over ("I am calm, I am calm, I am calm"), that's fine, too! I've found that what often works for me is just breathing softly and steadily and thinking only about my breathing. Soon, the constantly nagging thoughts in my brain begin to cease. I find my mind clearing. I realize I am in a state of *not-thinking*. Some people call this their "chair and stare" time. They just sit and *do* nothing at all for ten or fifteen minutes. They might *imagine* watching a beautiful sunset over the ocean, or they picture a rainbow after a spring storm. They might imagine themselves sitting in a large room, being cradled by God. He's not talking to them, and they're not talking either. They're just being held and comforted.

In this calm and serenity—in this atmosphere of peace—

you will be able to remember that you are a spiritual being as much as a physical one. You will be able to remember that you have been given special qualities. You are able to remember what is important to you in your life. In this case, silence really is golden.

If you are having trouble slowing down your mind during your rest stop, then you might try writing in what I call a Feelings Journal. In a notebook, write down some positive feelings you have about life, or read a passage from an inspirational book. You might try repeating a few lines from an inspiring poem. We forget about the power of simple poetry. Try Tennyson or Keats or Shakespeare or Robert Frost—anyone who has written something that in a couple of lines captures a feeling of emotional well-being.

I also recommend that you have your own getaway place—an area just for you to be alone with yourself. Some might have an extra bedroom. Others might use a spot in the garden or even in a closet. I recommend taking a long, hot bubble bath with lighted candles beside the bathtub. Take as long as you want. Concentrate only on the soothing tranquillity of the water. Your own private space gives you a chance to appreciate your own uniqueness and to renew your mind, body, and spirit!

The second kind of rest stop for you to make is one that involves "play." Do you remember when you were a child and how ready you were to go outside and play after school was over? Playing was a way you revitalized yourself in childhood. It boosted your mood and filled you with energy and prepared you for the next day.

As adults, we think we don't need to "play" as we did when we were children. We think we are too busy, too serious, and too responsible for play. Many of us not only have forgotten how to have fun, but we actually avoid having fun.

I know women who feel they don't deserve to put "play-time" in their life. They're having so much trouble balancing their roles as wife, mother, friend, sister, neighbor, and worker that something has to give—and usually that one thing is personal play.

It's the very attitude of play that can make us winners. Those of us with playful attitudes are more eager to try new things, to enjoy life, and to remain positive even during the down days. Instead of acting overburdened with responsibility, we approach every day with spontaneity. We become fuller human beings because we will be more likely, through play, to connect with that gloriously creative side of ourselves that can write, paint, sing, laugh, dance, and tell stories. When we are joyously at play, our body releases endorphins, a secretion from the brain that literally causes a biochemical change in our body. We become more relaxed, more cheerful, more content.

Clearly, play is a primary need in life—and the nice thing about it is that it is not defined in one particular way. Play for one person might be reading a novel while sitting in a rocker. For another person, it could be playing tennis. For another, it could be going to football games or it could even be watching dreamy, romantic movies. Swimming, shopping, walking—the list is endless. **Play is what makes you smile!**

Play is also vital for your sanity. If you don't occasionally let out the playful little girl who's inside you, she will eventually start kicking and screaming and throwing a tantrum that will come out one way or another. This happens because if you have not put playtime into your schedule, you may start experiencing anger and irritation. You can become like a stewpot about to boil over.

Doctors are recognizing the importance of play. Eleven

years ago, a family member of mine was being treated for an alcohol addiction at a treatment center in Arizona. I went as part of "family week." After a therapist there had talked to me for a few days, she realized I had been the "fixer" in the family—the one who had tried to fix everything when there was a problem. Upon hearing that I had been cleaning the house and cooking for myself since the age of nine, the therapist gently asked me: "Jinger, do you know how to play?"

"What?" I asked.

"Play," she said. "You've been acting like an adult since you were a little girl. Have you ever just relaxed and played?"

I realized I hadn't—so they taught me to play. I was encouraged to carry a doll around with me at all times, and at meetings I had to talk about her. I also was encouraged to play children's games, like hide-and-seek.

It turned out that I couldn't have had better therapy. I learned to let my "little girl" out to play and I felt astonishingly free! Today, I make sure all my rest stops include some playtime. Indeed, I make sure to stop and smell the roses whenever I get the chance. As much as I have a burning desire to be successful, I know that sanity and success go together. While not diverting my sight from my goals, I still know I must experience balance. I must rest, I must play, I must continually develop my own spiritual side. I want to spend plenty of time with my family, and I want to maintain my friendships. If the wheels of my life are not balanced, I know I am just one turn away from a crash. If I try to live a life of extremes, then I know I am going to be swerving too far in one direction.

Why don't you try it right now? Give yourself a break and take a rest stop. Spend the afternoon at the rest stop, if you choose. Stop consciously thinking about your self-improvement and do little things that will make you smile. Make your life beautiful. Act "as if" you don't have a problem in this world. You have been working very hard through this entire book—and you deserve to relax!

The New Positively You

You're a Miracle—Enjoy the Journey

The well-lived life is not a destination, but a process. If we are following what we have learned about ourselves, then change will come fast enough. Our negative attitudes are disappearing, our destructive behaviors are fading away—and we are freeing our true self that has been locked away for years.

NOW I AM GOING TO ASK YOU A SLIGHT VARIATION OF THE SAME question I asked at the very start of this book.

How does it feel to believe in yourself again?

Think about it. . . . Take a deep breath, clear your mind, and ask yourself: **How does it feel to be a different person?**

It's an astonishing feeling, isn't it? Perhaps you weren't aware of how, as you've been reading along, your whole life has been changing. Your blinders have fallen off and you have seen a new world ahead. You have beaten back your fears and rediscovered your dearest dreams. And here's the most remarkable thing: **You're already on the road to making them come true!**

Can you feel it? Can you feel that new power rushing through your body? Can you feel the self-confidence surging like a great ocean wave? Do you realize you have begun to parlay your talents into the highest possible achievements? You're doing it right now! You have reconnected to that inner strength that will let you change whatever it is you want to change in your life. You have rediscovered your potential that for years has been lying dormant, buried somewhere in your unconscious. You are now embracing your dreams and actively working at living them instead of daydreaming about them.

Take another deep breath, and, as soon as you finish this sentence, close your eyes and feel that glorious, bone-deep feeling of hope!

You have let go of the past, you have let go of your old roles, and you have started advancing confidently in the direction of your dreams! You now appreciate how miraculous your life is and how unique you are! You now believe in the glorious possibilities of the future! To use the words of the cosmetics business, your inner makeover is beautiful!

The Joy of the Journey

OF COURSE, YOUR JOURNEY IS NOT COMPLETE. BUT REmember this very important point: **The well-lived life is not a destination, but a process.** The joy of an adventure is not in finishing, but in undertaking the journey itself. If we are following what we have learned about ourselves so far, then change will be coming fast enough. Our negative attitudes are disappearing, our destructive behaviors are fading away—and we are freeing our true self, which may have been locked away for years.

To put it another way: Be patient. Instead of trying to "force" yourself to be happy, recognize that happiness is the by-product of you living at your personal best. You are headed toward a remarkably rich and fulfilled existence.

In fact, what you'll discover is that as you make just a small change or two in one part of your life, you will be making changes in other parts of your life that you hadn't previously considered. I know a woman who had a simple goal of treating people better at work. She decided that the one thing she had to do was develop more energy during the day so she wouldn't get cranky. Soon, she began following a much healthier diet (which led to her losing weight), and she also started working out (which gave her energy that she had never had before). Within a year and a half, the woman had lost fifty pounds—and that wasn't even something she had planned to do! She had stopped drinking coffee and alcohol and she was off high-fat foods entirely. Moreover, she had such a feeling of confidence and self-worth that she got promoted! Again, she hadn't planned on getting a promotion. She just wanted to get along better with coworkers.

Was this woman particularly strong-willed? No. Did she have some inner drive that I hadn't seen often in other women? No. Was she wildly fanatical about staying on the right road? No! She was simply persistent about making some elementary changes—and the momentum of those changes led her to a transformation of her entire life!

In many ways, I often think of my own life's journey as the equivalent to my marathon race that I earlier described.

No one told me I had to enter the race. There was no set of circumstances that forced me into the event. I decided I wanted to attempt such a staggering challenge—*twenty-six miles of running!* I wasn't out to win, I wasn't desperate to be recognized for being among the leaders. I just wanted to prove to myself that I could do it!

At first, looking way off down the road, I thought there was no way I was going to reach my destination. The marathon seemed too grueling, too tiring. There was no point, I said, in trying so hard. But as I continued training, I learned to enjoy the effort. The more I trained, the more I *wanted* to train. I wanted to work hard. Yes, I could have quit anytime I wished. I knew I was not going to come in first place. But I began to love the challenge of seeing a commitment become a reality. Instead of worrying about the destination, I began to celebrate the slow, steady change.

And, slowly, that dedication began to pay off. The results weren't dramatic day by day. But over several months, after a certain amount of sacrifice, I realized I was going to do well. The old "me" had disappeared, and a new, more alive "me" had emerged.

So don't worry about the destination. Instead, celebrate the small changes that are taking place—one small change in your mental attitude, one small change in your diet, one small change in your work habits. Just continue to add small changes to your life. You might decide to get up earlier, to take less time at lunch during the workday, to read more inspirational books at night before you go to bed, to start a daily exercise journal, to begin practicing a few simple affirmations, to read your Personal Mission Statement and review your Goal List. As time goes on, these changes will become bigger—and the results will be far more tangible.

A Miracle Story

HERE IS THE FINAL LESSON I'D LIKE TO SHARE: **Start seeing and believing in miracles!**

First-time parents always say the same thing: "It's a miracle!"

Now, nothing since the beginning of time has changed. Children have been born for thousands of years. What changed was the new parents' attitude about the birth. They witnessed their child entering the world and exclaimed, "We participated in a miracle!"

Miracles are only about *paying attention!* It's mindfulness about a sunset, a birth, a bird, a flower, the ocean, a toddler learning to walk, and the way your body works—they are miracles!

Begin today paying attention to the miracles going on around you every day. Your body is a machine that is running amazingly well. You don't have to tell it to breathe or for its blood to pump through your veins. Amazing, isn't it? It's a miracle!

A great rabbi named Zedek teaches that every day we see something beautiful, hear something beautiful, say something beautiful, and do something beautiful! Zedek teaches us to turn the ho-hums of everyday life into the ahas!

I lovingly encourage you to look for the everyday miracles that are all around you.

And, finally, a story of a miracle lady.

Throughout this book, I have mentioned various women I have come across in my own journey, and I have not used their actual names in order to respect their privacy. But, as we conclude, I am going to tell you a story about another friend of mine. Her real name is Mary Evans.

Mary lives in the tiny Mississippi town of Saltillo, just

north of Tupelo. She had a normal, quiet childhood—her father was a cotton and dairy farmer—and when she grew up and married, she and her husband bought a home next to her parents. She studied to be a hairdresser, and her life in Saltillo seemed set.

In 1973, however, Mary began noticing that she was having trouble seeing at night. She was bumping into things and tripping over objects right in front of her. Doctors diagnosed her condition as retinitis pigmentosa—degeneration of the retina. They said she would have trouble seeing for the rest of her life—but that was it. Nobody expected Mary's sight to disappear entirely.

In October 1984, however, Mary's retinas deteriorated and she went blind. Completely blind. She could see no light whatsoever. Everything was pitch-black. And after studying her eyes, the doctors told her the damage was irreversible.

Imagine being able to see for most of your life and suddenly being thrown into absolute darkness, never again able to look upon anyone you knew or loved. For Mary, the shock was so severe that she was institutionalized in a psychiatric hospital for five months. She had constant panic attacks and she wept uncontrollably. She couldn't keep food down. She was afraid of getting out of her bed. She preferred to lie in her room in total silence, refusing even to let the nurses turn on the radio or television. "The only times I got out of my bed were those times when I got down on my knees to pray for a miracle," she told me. "My only comfort was when my daddy sat by my bed and read to me out of the Bible."

The miracle—or at least, the miracle she was asking for—never came. She stayed blind. She returned to her home in late 1985, where she regularly went to a center for blind people and became trained in Braille. Social workers taught her how to arrange and change her clothes so she always knew what she was wearing, how to clean house and iron and cook, how to find things in the refrigerator, and how to use a cane when she walked.

Nothing, however, seemed to cure her depression. Although Mary was never suicidal, she was so disheartened that she spent the next several years staying mostly in her home. She literally didn't know what to do with herself. In 1988, her sister, Roseanna Behrman, who lived just up the road in Tupelo, told her she had joined BeautiControl and was looking for new saleswomen to recruit.

"Recruit me," said a desperate Mary.

"Mary, I'm a brand-new Consultant myself," said Roseanna. "What would the BeautiControl executives in Dallas do if they heard I had signed up a blind person to sell cosmetics?"

For the next few years, Mary gradually improved her emotional outlook. For a few years, she worked with a blind child who lived in the county, but when that child left the area, Mary had nothing to do. About that time, her sister called again looking for new Consultants. Mary again told Roseanna that she could do the job. This time, Roseanna agreed.

On April 30, 1993, Mary Evans became an official BeautiControl Consultant. Talk about a challenge. A blind woman was going to attempt to tell other women that she knew how to make them "look" better. The essence of our business is what we call "clinics," during which the Consultant talks to a small group of women, shows them our line of cosmetics and nutritional supplements, and then allows them to try the products. How was Mary going to stand in front of a potential customer and say, "You look beautiful wearing that blush"? How was she going to find new customers, since she would be unable to approach people to tell them about BeautiControl?

When we heard about Mary at the Dallas offices, we said, "Good for her. If she wants to sell, more power to her." Mary had just as much right to start her own business and make a living as any other woman did. Still, she knew it was definitely a major gamble for her to undertake such a business. She and her husband were not wealthy by any stretch of the imagination. After she paid $150 for her sales kit, she had $30 left in her bank account.

When the sales kit arrived, she opened it, felt our products, and within minutes was on the phone. She called a friend and began talking about her new career. By the time she went to bed that night, she had sold $100 worth of products. Within two weeks, she had interviewed and signed up another woman to join our company as well.

As the months passed, word began trickling back to headquarters about this remarkable woman. She had created her own Braille order form. She had typed Braille labels for all her products. She had come up with her own series of questions for her customers to help her determine what kind of products they needed. She had her husband or mother drive her to women's houses so she could show them her product line. She called three new women every day to inform them about the BeautiControl career opportunity. And she even began holding demonstrations in her home. Some of the women who arrived had no idea Mary was blind. "Girl, come on in here," Mary would say. "You're about to have the best time of your life." One day, a salesperson came to Mary's front door to sell her insurance. Mary invited her inside, but they never once talked about insurance. Mary began showing her the array of products she sold. A couple of hundred dollars in sales later, the salesperson (turned customer) left Mary's home.

It soon became obvious that Mary Evans, regardless of her blindness, had turned herself into a stunningly good sales-woman—something no one would have predicted. As she would later tell me, the process of doing something that she thought was impossible became her road back to happiness. "I realized I didn't have to succumb to circumstance," she said. "I realized that I could overcome whatever obstacles were in my way, no matter how big they seemed. You know, I could have spent the rest of my life trapped by my blind-ness—and no one would have blamed me. No one would have said, 'Mary, you need to do something with yourself.' But when I made the decision to set my goals, to have the right attitude, to have faith and determination, and to make sacrifices to improve my life, I became a different person."

What Mary did was a true miracle. But it was all the more amazing because she *created* that miracle! She did it all her-self! She could have quit so many times along the way, but, as she put it, "I had a vision that I could make a difference. I might have been blind, but I stuck to that vision."

Indeed, she did. In October 1996, Mary Evans was named a Sales Director of BeautiControl—one of the highest honors earned by our salespeople who sell a substantial amount of products and share their opportunity with a large number of new Consultants. As part of the honor, she was given a brand-new Pontiac Grand Prix. The car was taken to a large, empty parking lot, and Mary got in behind the driver's seat. She turned on the ignition, put the car in drive, and inched forward. As she did so, she began to weep.

"I think at that moment, I was just so overwhelmed that I had made it," she later said. "I had spent years going through a depression that nearly killed me. I had been burdened with heartache and despair. Yet, I still was able to develop a pride in myself that I never knew was possible. If there's one thing I would pass on to others, it's to never lose that pride in yourself. All of us can do great things!"

If Mary Evans in Saltillo, Mississippi, can accomplish what she did, then who knows what will happen to you on your road? Who knows what glories await you? Who knows what kind of abundant miracles and joyous life you are about to discover?

You are headed toward a limitless horizon. I wish you Godspeed.